YEAR-ROUND
CRAFTS
FOR KIDS

YEAR-ROUND
CRAFTS
FOR KIDS

**Barbara L. Dondiego,
Illustrated by Jacqueline Cawley**

TAB | **TAB BOOKS**
Blue Ridge Summit, PA

FIRST EDITION
FOURTH PRINTING

© 1988 by **TAB BOOKS.**
TAB BOOKS is a division of McGraw-Hill, Inc.

Library of Congress Cataloging-in-Publication Data

Dondiego, Barbara L.
   Year-round crafts for kids / by Barbara L. Dondiego ; illustrated
by Jacqueline Cawley.
      p.   cm.
   Includes index.
   Summary: Provides instructions for over 100 inexpensive crafts,
both simple and complex; grouped by months of the year.
   ISBN 0-8306-0904-0 : ISBN 0-8306-2904-1 (pbk.) :
   1. Handicraft. [1. Handicraft.] I. Cawley, Jacqueline, ill.
II. Title.
TT157.D632 1987   87-19419
745.5—dc19   CIP
                                            AC

TAB BOOKS offers software for sale. For information and a catalog, please contact
TAB Software Department, Blue Ridge Summit, PA, 17294-0850.

Questions regarding the content of this book should be addressed to:

Reader Inquiry Branch
TAB BOOKS
Blue Ridge Summit, PA 17294-0850

Edited by Suzanne L. Cheatle
Designed by Jaclyn Boone
Half-title pages illustration by Danne Kennedy
Photographs: J. Wayne Bratten—Perfect Prints of Marietta, Georgia

Contents

To Dan, Terry, Barbara, Elizabeth, and Mary,
with love.

MOM'S BOOK

Where's my breakfast? Where should I look?
Quiet! Mommy's writing a book.
Help! I'm being chased by an alligator!
Quiet! Mom's talking to her illustrator.
I need clean clothes! Is there no Mom home?
Quiet! The publisher's on the 'phone.
This house is a mess and that's a fact.
Quiet! Mom's reading her book contract.
Mom! Mom! Our team! It won!
Come and tell me, Honey. The book is done.

How to Teach Your
Child by Making Crafts

1. Set aside an hour 5 days a week to create crafts with your child. If he can invite a friend to join him, it will be even more fun.

2. Let him pick out the craft he wants to make.

3. Check the Materials List for the craft. Buy what is needed. Also buy a package of tracing paper. It can be found in the school and office supplies section of grocery stores and drugstores.

4. Follow the directions for making the craft. It is very important to encourage your child to do as much of the work of making the craft as he possibly can. The more he cuts, the better he will get at it. The more he is told to hold his marker or crayon "the right way," the more accustomed to writing he will become. Learning preschool skills is truly a case of "practice makes perfect."

5. Talk to your child while he makes the craft. Tell him that the toilet-paper roll used to make the Circle Pig is a *cylinder*, for instance. Tell him to glue the *yellow rectangle* onto the cylinder to make Cylinder Bee. In this way he will learn what words mean through active manipulation of the colors, shapes, and sizes.

6. Praise your child for what he has created!

Acknowledgments

My special thanks to the delightful children whose photographs fill this book, and to their parents. The children are: Barbara Dondiego, Elizabeth Dondiego, Mary Dondiego, Kimberly Doucette, Michael Doucette, Mark Doucette, Maureen Cook, Elizabeth Cook, Alison Maclean, David Maclean, Keith Fraley, Lynn Fraley, Andrea Guthrie, Jennifer Guthrie, and Jean-Paul Fournier.

A special thanks, too, to the students and teachers of Murdock Elementary School.

Preface

This book reflects my experiences since the publication of *Crafts for Kids: A Month-By-Month Idea Book*. Of the last three years, one was spent teaching in an academically oriented pre-school to prevent my family from starving. There I developed crafts for three-, four-, and five-year-olds. The next two years were spent as a volunteer in public school with eight-, nine-, and ten-year-olds.

I wish I could say that the ten-year-olds and I spent many pleasurable hours creating crafts together, but actually it was all I could do to survive every time I walked into their classroom. Ten-year-olds are especially hard to please since they like to add their own input to everything and one of their favorite phrases is "Who cares," which is spoken as a statement, not a question. They'll hoot you right out of the room and throw empty milk cartons at you if the craft idea is not to their liking. Old-fashioned respect has largely disappeared in ten-year-olds. Eventually we came up with some good ideas that suited all of us, including the child who felt compelled to make every craft look like "Bill the Cat." We even learned to enjoy making crafts together. At least, I think we did.

Kathy Nichols' fourth-grade class of eight- and nine-year-olds was fun to teach. After each art project, they wrote thank-you notes, which were graded by their teacher before being sent to me. I have included some of them in this book just as I received them, except I left out the wrinkles and the smudges. Hopefully your children will enjoy the crafts in this book just as much as they did.

Introduction

This craft book is filled with over 100 inexpensive ideas that adults can use with children from ages two to ten. It is written for any adult who wants to help a child become more creative and imaginative. It will teach children that there are wonderful things they can do with their spare time besides watch television.

Year-Round Crafts for Kids is easy to use. Each craft includes a list of needed materials, plus precise, step-by-step directions and simple, traceable patterns. It contains 100 illustrations by Jacqueline Cawley, the remarkably precise artist who illustrated my first book, *Crafts for Kids: A Month-By-Month Idea Book*. She draws the crafts so realistically that it's easy to tell what the finished product will look like.

All the crafts can be completed in less than an hour, requiring little of a busy adult's time. The book is useful for scout leaders, classroom teachers, day-care providers, grandparents, pediatric hospitals, and busy parents who want to spend quality time with their children. It's a terrific rainy-day and resource book for wherever children are staying.

Not only are the crafts useful, decorative, and fun to make, but most of them are made out of practically nothing. They are created by the children from things found in grocery stores and drugstores, such as construction paper and glue, cotton balls, paper plates and bags, and muffin-cup liners. Many are made from castoffs that we bring into our homes and throw away, such as walnut shells, toilet-paper rolls, baby-food jars, and empty salt boxes.

Some of the crafts, designed especially for preschoolers, are simple to make. Many have moving parts to make them more interesting. Other crafts are suitable for older children, eight years old and up, who like to create and improvise. Several crafts teach children of all ages to develop construction skills by using geometric shapes. Paper cylinders and cones are made by the children, then put together as three-dimensional objects that stand by themselves or hang up in a decorative way.

Children enjoy making things. Once they discover that they really can make something nice out of an old orange juice can or a seed pod from a Sweet Gum tree, their imaginations fly into top gear. Craft time is not mindless busy work. When children work with crafts, they learn to see possibilities and alternatives that were not visible to them before. They develop better fine-motor coordination as they assemble small art objects; they learn to follow directions and to work in sequence; and they learn to complete their projects. The finished products are treated like crown jewels by the proud children who make them.

This book shows children how to get started. Just add a few items to your grocery list, grab the scissors and glue, and make something with your children. They'll love it as they learn.

JANUARY CRAFTS

The year begins with a party hat covered with New Year's resolutions. My resolutions always include something about losing weight.

To keep our January resolutions about dieting, we're not supposed to feed ourselves very much. At least the children can feed the birds outside with a Pine-Cone Bird Feeder.They can make a snowman without using snow, and they can fill the house with the wonderful aroma of baking bread as mother and father drool. Then they can spend the cold days inside making Peanutty Brittle, which is nutritious, and creating with salt boxes, which they have emptied onto the icy stoop.

NEW YEAR'S HAT AND KAZOO

The children can begin the New Year right by making resolutions (such as helping with the household chores). Then they can make a kazoo so they can toot their horn!

AGE GROUP

Children from ages 3 to 8 will enjoy this craft.

MATERIALS LIST

Each child needs:
◇ 1 large sheet of construction paper 12″ x 18″
◇ Construction paper in bright colors
◇ A pencil
◇ A ruler
◇ Scissors
◇ Glue
◇ 2 pieces of ribbon 15″ each
◇ A paper punch
◇ A toilet-paper roll
◇ Markers or crayons
◇ A piece of wax paper 4″ x 4″
◇ A rubber band

DIRECTIONS FOR THE HAT

Give the children the following directions: "Hold the large sheet of construction paper horizontally by its two top corners. Pull your two hands together and downward, overlapping the edges of the paper until it comes to a sharp point at the top. Glue the cone to make it hold its shape.

"Cut off the pointed bottom so the hat will stand up.

"Use the pencil and ruler to draw a rectangle 5 x 6 inches on bright construction paper. Cut out the rectangle.

"Fringe the rectangle along one 6-inch side. Apply a thick line of glue to the bottom of the fringe and wrap the fringe around the pointed top of the hat. Bend the fringes outward a little to make a tassle on the hat.

"Decorate the hat with promises to help your mother and father. Write the promises on pieces of paper and glue them to the hat. Some ideas are to sweep the porch, set the table, or feed the cat.

"Make pictures for your promises from colored paper. For instance, make a paper bowl of cat food, and glue it to your hat. Cut out a construction paper plate, knife, fork, and spoon, and glue them on the hat if they have promised to set the table.

"Punch a hole in each side of the hat near the bottom. Insert a 15-inch ribbon in each hole. Tie a big knot inside the hat so the ribbon will not pull through the hole. Put the hat on and tie it under your chin."

DIRECTIONS FOR THE KAZOO

Instruct the children as follows: "Use the pencil and ruler to draw a paper rectangle 4½ x 6 inches. Cut out the rectangle and spread glue on it. Wrap the rectangle around the roll, covering the roll completely.

"Decorate the kazoo with crayons or markers.

"Cut a 4-inch square from wax paper. Fit the wax paper over one end of the kazoo. Fasten it in place loosely with a rubber band. Punch a small hole in the middle of the wax paper with a sharp pencil. Pull the edge of the wax paper upward, so your hands will not touch it.

"Place the roll against your mouth. Sing or talk into the kazoo. The wax paper will vibrate and your voice will be louder."

PINE-CONE BIRD FEEDER

This is a simple feeder, not too messy, that attracts the tufted titmouse, chickadee, cardinal, blue jay, and finch, among others.

AGE GROUP

Children of all ages can help make this feeder. Preschoolers learn to spread with a knife and to tie the ribbon onto the pine cone. Birds and squirrels of all ages also like this craft.

MATERIALS LIST

Each child needs:
◇ A pine cone
◇ Ribbon or strong string
◇ Wax paper
◇ ¼ cup peanut butter
◇ ¼ cup bread crumbs (Make your own from bread scraps.)
◇ 1 cup bird seed (Grocery stores sell it.)
◇ A large bowl
◇ A wooden spoon

DIRECTIONS

Give the children the following instructions: "Tie the ribbon or string near the top of the pine cone so it can be hung. Lay the pine cone on wax paper. "Measure the peanut butter and bread crumbs into the bowl. Mix with a wooden spoon until smooth. Spread this mixture on the pine cone. Roll the pine cone in bird seed. Press more seed between the scales of the pine cone. Hang the Pine-Cone Bird Feeder outside where you can see it from a window.

PAPER-PLATE WATCHBIRD

This is a Watchbird that watches the children's rooms, saying, *WELCOME* or *PLEASE KNOCK*, whenever they choose.

AGE GROUP

The Watchbird helps children learn cutting, gluing, writing, and construction skills. It's a fun craft for children 3 through 9.

MATERIALS LIST

Each child needs:
◇ Four 9″ white paper plates (Buy the cheapest generic plates.)
◇ A pencil
◇ Scissors
◇ Glue
◇ Light-colored poster paint
◇ A Styrofoam meat tray
◇ A sponge cut into a 2″ square
◇ A black marker
◇ Brown and yellow construction paper
◇ A paper punch
◇ Crimped paper ribbon

DIRECTIONS

Instruct the children as follows: "Use the pattern to draw a circle head in the center of a paper plate. Use the other patterns to draw two wings and a tail on another paper plate.

"Pour a small amount of poster paint onto the Styrofoam meat tray. Cover your work surface with newspaper and put on a painting coat.

"Wet the sponge square. Dip it into the paint. Gently dab the paper plates with an up-and-down motion. The imprint of the sponge should be visible on the plate. This process of painting is called *stippling*.

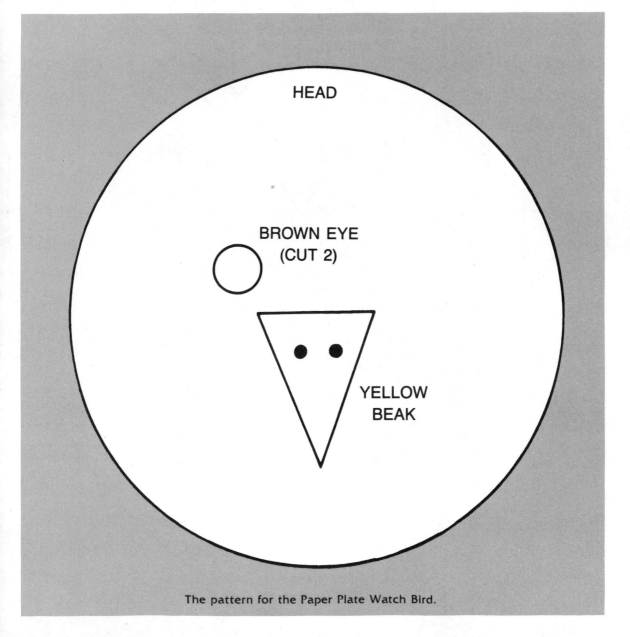

HEAD

BROWN EYE
(CUT 2)

YELLOW
BEAK

The pattern for the Paper Plate Watch Bird.

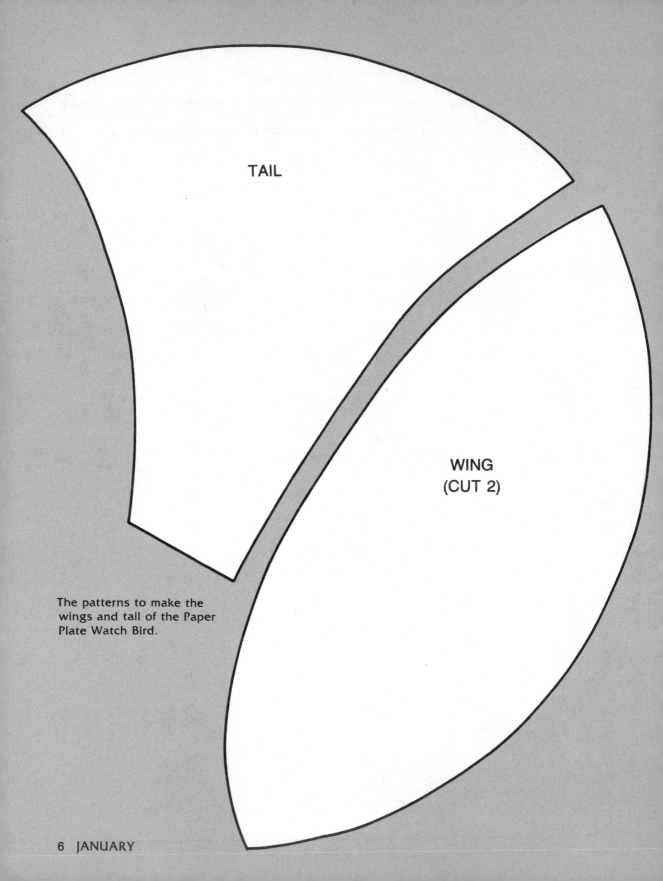

TAIL

WING
(CUT 2)

The patterns to make the wings and tail of the Paper Plate Watch Bird.

"Stipple the bottoms of the two remaining plates. They form the body of the bird."

After the paint dries tell the children: "Cut out the head, two wings, and tail. Put the two whole plates together, bottoms out. Spread glue around their edges. Insert the head and tail between the two plates, press the edges of the plates gently together, adding more glue if necessary.

"With a black marker, print WELCOME on one wing and PLEASE KNOCK on the other. Glue one wing on one side of the bird, in the middle of the body, and one wing on the other side.

"Use the patterns to draw two eyes on brown construction paper and a triangle beak on yellow paper. Cut out the pieces. Glue them on one side of the head.

"Add eyeballs, eyelashes, eyebrows, and nostril holes with black marker. Use the paper punch to punch a hole in the top of the body, through both plates. Insert a 16-inch piece of ribbon and tie it into a circle.

"Print your name on your Watchbird. Hang him on the doorknob of your room."

WOOLIE-PULLIE

Give each child a Styrofoam meat tray to hold cut-out
craft pieces, and to keep glue off tabletops.

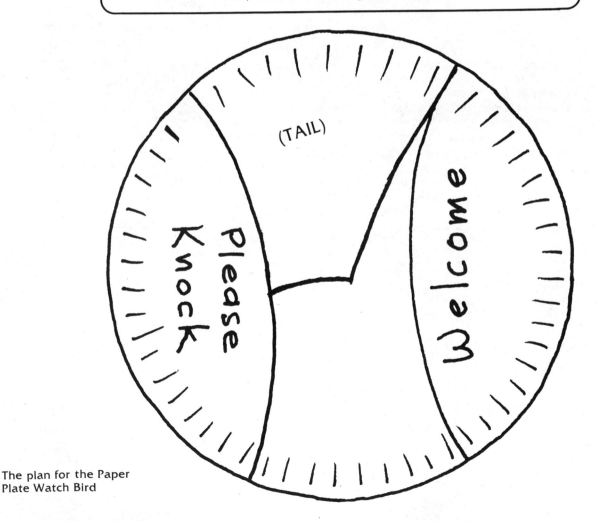

The plan for the Paper
Plate Watch Bird

THREE-FACED SNOWMAN

This snowman has three faces, depending on which way he's turned. Make all the faces look alike, or make each one different.

AGE GROUP

Children as young as 2 can make this snowman with help from an adult. The craft will interest older children because it teaches them an interesting construction skill.

MATERIALS LIST

Each child needs:
◇ A pencil
◇ Scissors
◇ Glue
◇ Black, white, red, and orange construction paper

DIRECTIONS

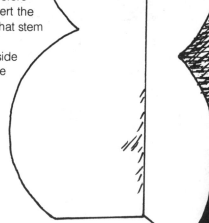

Give the children the following instructions: "Fold two pieces of white construction paper in half. Use the pattern to trace the snowman shape onto both pieces of paper. Make sure the flat side of the pattern is laying along the fold of the paper. Cut the patterns out through the double thickness of paper. When the cutouts are unfolded, you will have two whole snowmen.

"Trace the hat onto a double thickness of black construction paper. Cut out two hats. Fold the hats (as shown on the pattern). Apply glue to half of each hat, plus the hat stem. Press the glued sides together so they match.

"Apply glue to half of each snowman (as shown on the pattern). Press the glued sides together so they match. Before the glue dries, pull the two sides apart at the top and insert the stem of the hat. Press the two sides together again, with the hat stem place between them.

"Make three faces for the snowman—a face for each side of him. Cut out eyes, nose, and a mouth for each face. One face can look smiling and happy, one face can look sad, and one face can be asleep."

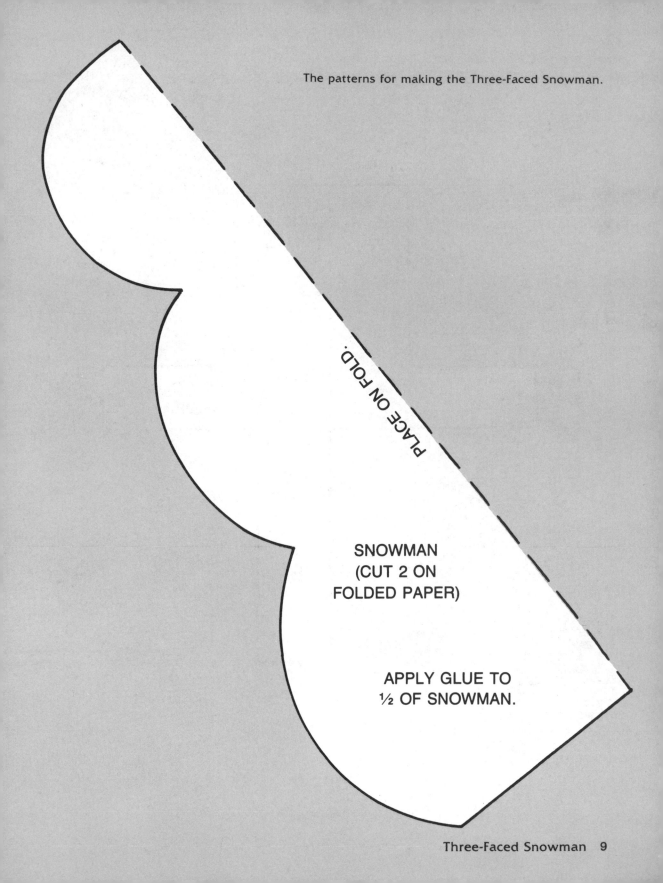

The patterns for making the Three-Faced Snowman.

PLACE ON FOLD.

SNOWMAN
(CUT 2 ON
FOLDED PAPER)

APPLY GLUE TO
½ OF SNOWMAN.

The patterns for making the Three-Faced Snowman.

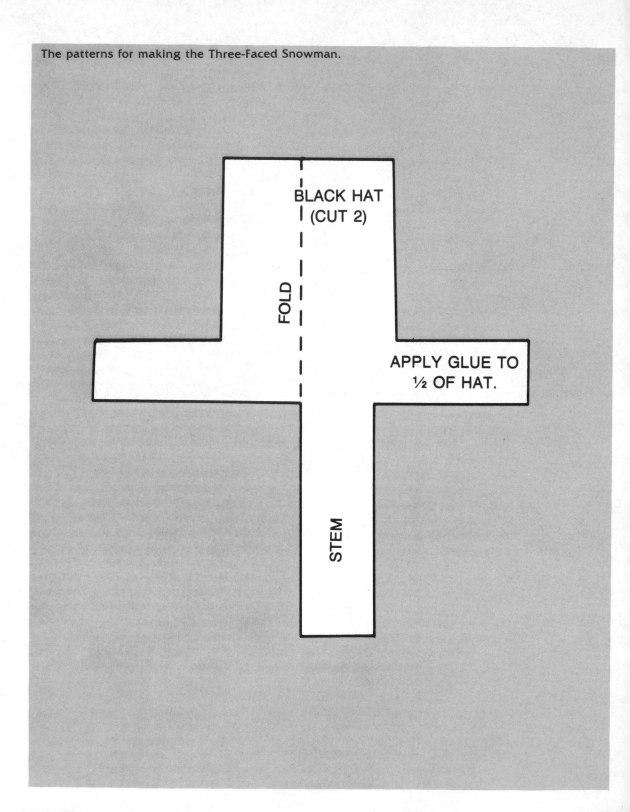

BLACK HAT
(CUT 2)

FOLD

APPLY GLUE TO
½ OF HAT.

STEM

HANG-UP SNOWMAN

Hang-Up Snowman is a fluffy reminder that spring is not just around the corner.

AGE GROUP

Children from ages 2 through 8 will enjoy tracing, cutting, and gluing this craft.

MATERIALS LIST

Each child needs:
◇ A pencil
◇ Scissors
◇ Glue
◇ Cardboard, such as poster paper
◇ Cotton balls
◇ Black and red construction paper
◇ A paper punch
◇ Yarn
◇ Black felt (optional)

DIRECTIONS

Instruct the children as follows: "Use the pattern to trace the snowman onto the cardboard. Cut out the pattern. Trace the hat onto black construction paper or black felt. Cut out two hats and make a hole in the top of each with the paper punch.

"Spread glue on one side of the snowman. Cover him with pieces of cotton. Repeat this to cover the other side with cotton.

"Glue one hat on his head. Glue the other hat on the other side of his head. Then glue the hats together at the top. Tie a piece of yarn through the hole to hang up the snowman.

"Use the paper punch to make two black paper eyes and three black paper buttons. Punch out a red paper nose. Cut a red mouth in the shape of a smile. Glue them onto the snowman's face.

The patterns for the Hang-Up Snowman.

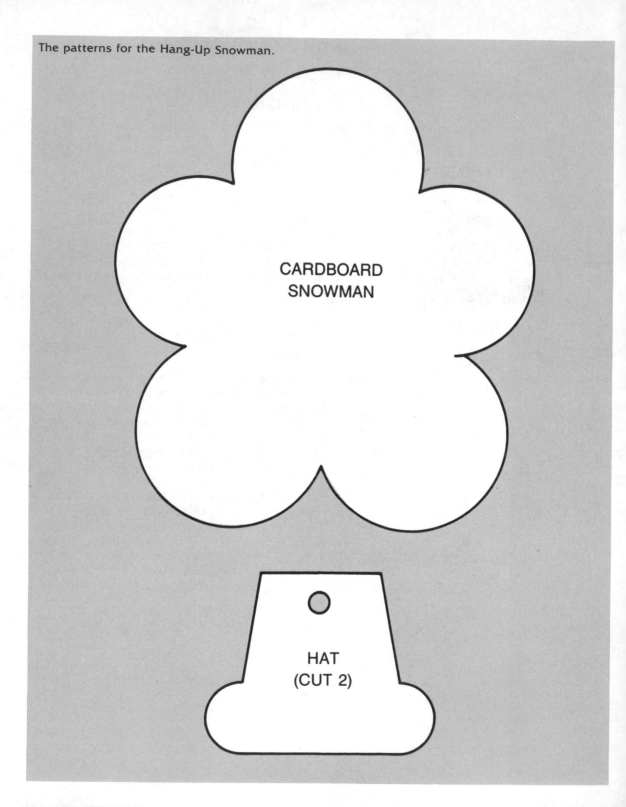

CARDBOARD
SNOWMAN

HAT
(CUT 2)

SNOWMAN PICTURE

The frame for this picture is the lid from a large jar of peanut butter.

AGE GROUP

Children ages 2 through 6 will enjoy making this craft.

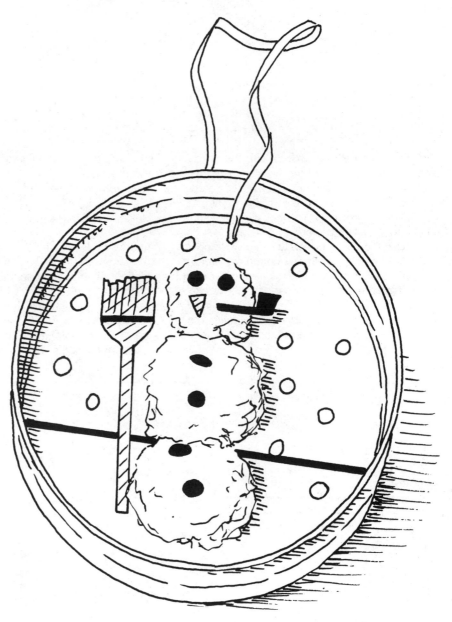

MATERIALS LIST

Each child needs:
◇ A large jar lid (I used one that is 4½" in diameter.)
◇ A pencil
◇ Blue, black, white, and orange construction paper
◇ Scissors
◇ Glue
◇ A black marker
◇ A paper punch
◇ 3 cotton balls
◇ A hammer
◇ A nail
◇ 10" ribbon or string for hanging

DIRECTIONS

Instruct the children as follows: "Use the jar lid as a pattern, and trace a circle onto blue construction paper. Cut out the pattern. Glue the circle inside the lid.

"Use the black marker to draw a line across the circle, from one side to the other. Glue three cotton balls on the blue circle so they look like a snowman.

"Add two eyes and four buttons to the snowman. Make them with the paper punch and black construction paper.

"Use the paper punch to make white construction paper circles. Glue as many as you want on the blue paper around the snowman to look like snowflakes.

"Add a tiny orange triangle nose to the snowman's face. Use the pattern to trace a pipe onto black construction paper. Trace a broom onto orange paper. Fringe the wide part of the broom to make it look like broom straws. Draw a black line across the broom to look like stitching. Glue the pipe on the snowman's mouth. Glue the broom next to the snowman.

"With a hammer and nail, pound a hole through the lid at the top of the picture. Insert a ribbon or string for hanging. Hang the Snowman Picture on a doorknob to decorate for winter."

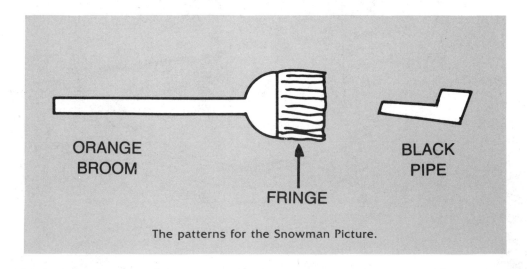

ORANGE BROOM

FRINGE

BLACK PIPE

The patterns for the Snowman Picture.

SALT-BOX PIG

When my third-grade friends made the Salt-Box Pig, they furnished their own salt boxes easily enough, but the hard part was getting them to bring a cork for the pig's snout. One child brought a screw-on cap from a wine bottle. Another brought a cork from a bottle of champagne. It was so fat it took up the pig's entire face. A third child brought half a cork. He said his mom and dad bought a bottle of wine just so he could bring the cork to school. They broke the cork in half while trying to get it out of the bottle. I gave him a whole cork. Too late I found out that hardware stores sell #15 corks, which make real good pig snouts. Here are two of the thank-you notes the children sent me.

Dear Mrs. Dondiego,

Thank you for makeing the pig with us. My dogs allways looks at it. I had fun makeing it to. Art is a barul of fun. My pig's nose is inside him to.

Love, Jonathan

Dear Mrs. Dondiego,

I had a great! time. I am going to use my pig for deckaration. Because I don't know where to put it. Right now it just sits there. And it looks like he is going to the bathroom because he can't stand up anymore, because at Brownies his legs kina got bent. Great pig!

Your friend, Christy

Like Christy says, this is a great pig.

AGE GROUP

With adult help, even preschoolers can make this pig. It can be turned into a bank, which is popular with children as old as 10.

MATERIALS LIST

For each child you need:
◇ A pencil
◇ A ruler
◇ An empty salt box with a spout
◇ Orange, black, and white construction paper
◇ A cork from a wine bottle, or a #15 cork
◇ A black marker or pen
◇ A 6″ piece of narrow paper ribbon
◇ Scissors
◇ Glue
◇ A paper punch
◇ You also need a sharp knife.

DIRECTIONS

Instruct the children as follows: "Use the pencil and ruler to draw a rectangle 5½ × 12 inches on orange construction paper. Cut out the rectangle. Measure and draw four rectangles 2½ × 3½ inches each on orange construction paper. Cut them out.

"Trace around the end of the salt box on orange paper to make two orange circles. Cut out the circles. Use the pattern to trace and cut out two orange ears, two red circle cheeks, and two white circle eyes.

"Apply glue to the large orange rectangle. Wrap the rectangle around the salt box, completely covering it. Apply glue to the two orange circles. Glue one on each end of the salt box."

FOR ADULTS ONLY: Use the sharp knife to cut around the salt spout, right through the paper covering it. Pry the spout open carefully, leaving paper on it to cover the metal piece. The spout is the pig's mouth.

Then tell the children: "To make feet, roll each of the smaller orange rectangles into cylinders 2½ inches long. Overlap them and glue the edges so they will keep their shape. Draw four 1-inch slits down one end of each cylinder. Space them equally apart. Cut the slits and spread them out to form four tabs.

"Put glue on the tabs. Stick the cylinder feet on the bottom of the pig to make front and back feet. Press on the tabs until they stay in place.

"Apply glue to the rounded top of the two orange ears. Glue them on both sides of the head with the tips of the ears pointed down."

FOR ADULTS ONLY: To make the snout, use a sharp knife or the pointed tip of a pair of scissors to make a hole in the pig's face, ¼ to ½ inch above the mouth. Rotate the knife or scissors to make a hole that is slightly smaller than the cork. Gently force the cork into the hole so that it sticks there. The children can draw two nostril holes on the cork with a black pen or marker.

Then continue your instructions to the children: "Glue two white circle eyes on the pig's face. Add two black circle eyeballs, made with the paper punch. Glue on two red circle cheeks.

"Draw on eyelashes and eyebrows. Draw cloven hooves with a black marker. Curl the paper ribbon with the edge of the scissors. Glue it on to make a tail."

FOR ADULTS ONLY: Cut a 1-inch slit in the back of the pig to make it into a bank. Pennies and dimes can also be deposited through the pig's mouth.

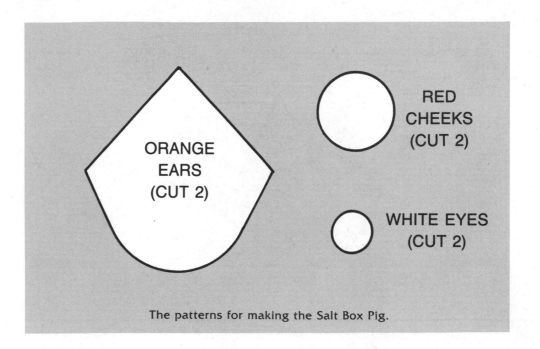

The patterns for making the Salt Box Pig.

SALT-BOX ROCKET

This craft gives the children a hands-on experience with geometric shapes, because the rocket has a cone nose and cylinder jets. It can be turned into a bank, too. Once the money is put in the rocket, it will not come out. It's a great way to save.

AGE GROUP

This is a good craft for children 6 years old and up. Younger children can make it with a lot of adult help.

MATERIALS LIST

For each child you need:

◇ A pencil
◇ A ruler
◇ An empty salt box
◇ Yellow and blue construction paper
◇ Scissors
◇ Glue
◇ Stars (from the School Supplies section of grocery and drug stores)
◇ You also need a sharp knife.

DIRECTIONS

Give the following directions to the children: "Use a pencil and ruler to measure a rectangle 5½ × 12 inches on blue construction paper. Cut the rectangle out. Measure and cut out four blue rectangles 2½ × 3½ inches. Trace around the end of the salt box to make a circle on blue construction paper. Cut the circle out, too."

You do the measuring and cutting for younger children, but encourage those 6 years old and older to try for themselves. They'll learn a lot by doing.

Instruct the children: "Use the pattern to trace the two cone holders and the cone onto yellow construction paper. Cut them out.

"Apply glue to the large blue rectangle. Wrap the rectangle around the salt box, completely covering it. Apply glue to the blue circle. Glue it on one end of the salt box. This is the bottom of the rocket.

"Roll each of the small blue rectangles into cylinders 2½ inches long. These are the rocket's four jets. Overlap them and glue the edges so they will keep their shape. Draw four 1-inch slits down one end of each cylinder; space them equally apart. Cut the slits and spread them out to form four tabs.

"Put glue on these tabs. Glue all four cylinders to the bottom of the rocket. Trim the tabs if they hang over the edge of the bottom too far.

"Measure and cut out a strip of yellow construction paper ¾ × 12 inches. Glue it around the bottom edge of the rocket.

"Apply glue to the rounded edge of the two cone holders. Press them on the sides of the rocket, opposite one another and extending over the top edge. Apply glue to the holders and slip the cone over them to form the pointed nose of the rocket.

"To form the cone, hold the cone cutout with the flat edge at the top. Holding it at each point, pull your two hands together and downward. Overlap the edges until the paper comes to a sharp point at the top, and the bottom of the cone fits on the top of the rocket. Glue the cone to make it hold its shape.

"Apply glue to the outside of the cone holders. Slip the cone over these holders so that it sits on top of the rocket and hangs over the edge slightly.

"Add stars all over the rocket. Make an American flag by cutting white paper into a small rectangle 1 × 1¾ inches. Draw stars and stripes on it and glue it onto the nose cone."

The letters *USA* were added to this rocket. We cut them out of construction paper, but the children can draw them on the rocket with a marker. To turn the rocket into a bank, cut a 1-inch slit in the side of it with a sharp knife.

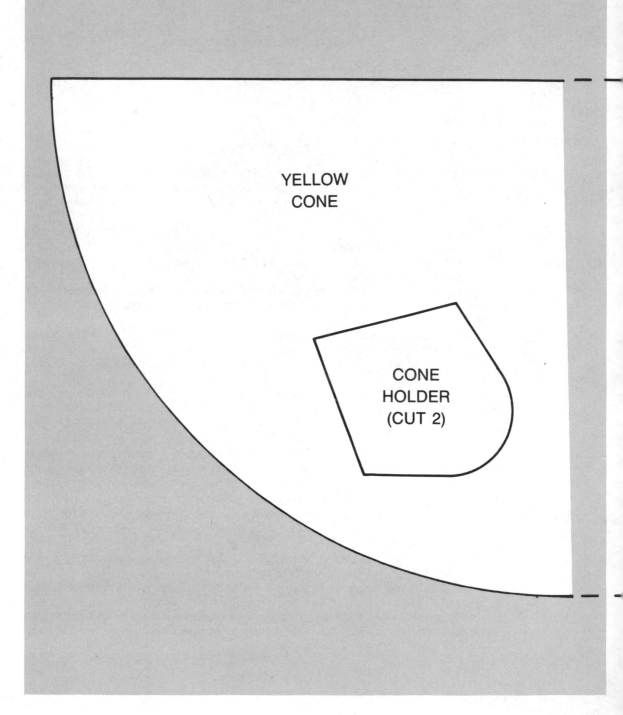

YELLOW
CONE

CONE
HOLDER
(CUT 2)

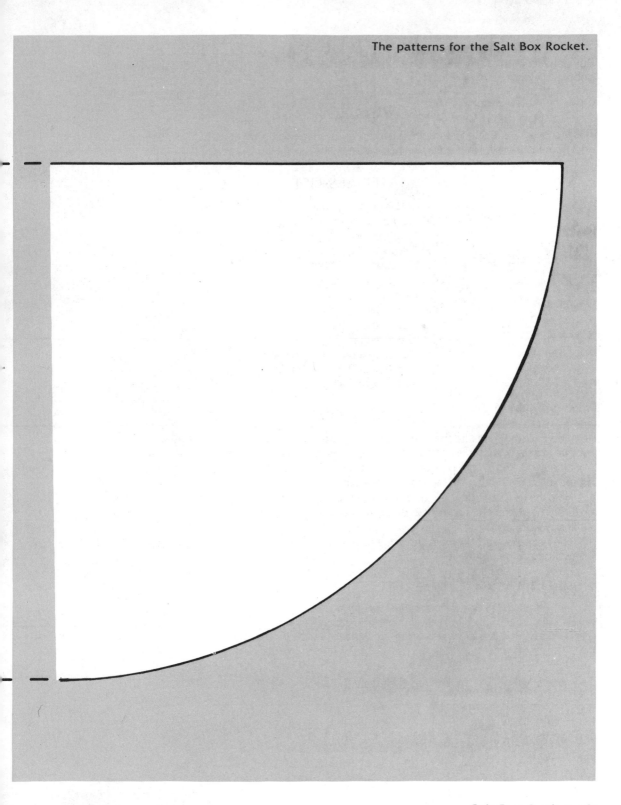

BRAN MUFFINS

Buy generic raisin bran if possible, or use any bran cereal that your children won't eat. They'll gobble up these muffins and never know.

AGE GROUP

This is a delicious recipe for all ages. Children 2 years old and up will learn to follow directions, and to measure, stir, and bake.

MATERIALS LIST

◇ A 12-cup muffin pan
◇ Solid shortening
◇ A large bowl
◇ A wooden spoon
◇ 1½ cups raisin bran cereal
◇ 1 cup milk
◇ 1 egg
◇ ¼ cup oil
◇ 1 cup flour
◇ ½ cup sugar
◇ 2½ teaspoons baking powder
◇ ½ teaspoon baking soda
◇ ½ teaspoon salt

DIRECTIONS

Help the children measure the cereal, milk, egg, and oil into a large bowl. They should stir it with a wooden spoon. Let it stand for 5 minutes to soften the cereal.

Meanwhile, the children can grease the muffin cups, using their fingers and solid shortening. Wipe excess shortening off the sides of the cups.

Help the children add the flour, sugar, baking powder, baking soda, and salt to the cereal mixture. They should stir it until it is barely mixed and is still lumpy. If they stir too much, the muffins will be tough.

They should use a ¼ measuring cup to dip the batter into the muffin cups. Have them fill each cup three-fourths full.

Bake in a preheated oven at 400° F for about 20 minutes, or until the muffins are golden brown. Eat hot or cold.

PEANUTTY BRITTLE

At last, here's a candy that you won't mind your children eating! Peanutty Brittle has as much protein and B vitamins as a peanut butter sandwich.

AGE GROUP

Adults must do the cooking, but all children will love to do the eating. Let the children help by measuring, greasing the pan, and eating the balls of candy that you test for doneness.

MATERIALS LIST

◇ 1 cup sugar
◇ ½ cup corn syrup
◇ ½ cup water
◇ 2 cups salted cocktail peanuts
◇ 1 tablespoon butter
◇ ½ teaspoon baking soda
◇ A 3-quart saucepan
◇ A wooden spoon
◇ A greased cookie sheet

DIRECTIONS

Help the children measure the sugar, corn syrup, and water into the saucepan. Bring this mixture to a boil over high heat, then reduce the heat to medium. Let the candy simmer, stirring occasionally, until it reaches the soft-ball stage (238° F on a candy thermometer). Test for this stage of doneness by dropping a small amount of the candy into a bowl of cold water. Feel the candy with your fingers. When it can be shaped into a soft ball, it is ready.

Stir in the peanuts. Continue cooking over medium heat, stirring constantly, until the candy forms a hard ball when dropped into cold water (290 ° F on a candy thermometer). It will reach this last stage very quickly.

Remove the saucepan from the heat. Stir in the butter. Then add the baking soda and gently stir until the candy foams a little and turns a light color. The baking soda creates millions of tiny bubbles, which make the candy tender.

Spread the Peanutty Brittle on the greased cookie sheet. Let it cool 1 hour. Loosen it from the sheet with a spatula. Break it into pieces and store it in an airtight container.

FEBRUARY
CRAFTS

During this month, which in most parts of the country is a good time to stay indoors, the children can have a Paper Bag Piñata Party. They can clean up their room and store toys in Egg-Carton Toy Bins. They'll discover that empty toilet-paper rolls should never be thrown away, and they can sit at the kitchen table sewing doily balls while mother struggles to make supper.

PAPER-BAG PIÑATA

This new version of a holiday piñata is much easier to make than a traditional one. In fact, it's so easy, even a child can do it!

AGE GROUP

Children from ages 5 to 10 will enjoy making and decorating the Paper-Bag Piñata. Fill it with goodies that are individually wrapped.

MATERIALS LIST

◇ A paper grocery bag
◇ A paper punch
◇ Narrow crimped paper ribbon
◇ 2 rolls of crepe-paper streamers in 2 different colors
◇ Scissors
◇ Glue
◇ Scraps of brightly colored construction paper
◇ Candy, toys, books, and cookies
◇ A plastic baseball bat
◇ A blindfold

DIRECTIONS

Instruct the children as follows. You might want to have each of them do only one step, or take turns.

"Open the grocery bag. Fold down the top toward the inside about 3 inches. Make four holes with the paper punch in the top of the bag, one hole on each side.

"Tie a 24-inch ribbon through each hole. Tie the four ribbons together above the bag to make a handle.

"Cut the crepe paper into pieces that are long enough to fit around the grocery bag.

"Starting at the bottom, apply a thin line of glue completely around the bag. Glue on a crepe-paper streamer so it goes all the way around the bag.

"Apply another thin line of glue above this streamer. Glue on a second crepe-paper streamer of a different color, slightly overlapping the first one. It, too, should fit all the way around the bag.

"Continue to apply a line of glue above the streamers, gluing on the streamers one at a time until the bag is covered. Be sure to alternate the colors.

"Turn the bag upside down. Spread a thin layer of glue all over the bottom. Glue streamers to the bottom so they hang down. Add as many streamers as it takes to cover the bottom of the piñata.

"Turn the piñata right side up. Decorate it to look like a clown by cutting big eyes, nose, and mouth from brightly colored construction paper. Glue them on. Add big eyebrows and eyeballs made with the paper punch."

Hang the Paper-Bag Piñata up to dry overnight. Fill it with wrapped soft candy, individual bags of fruit, toys, cookies, books, or whatever the children will enjoy.

Hang the piñata up high, or have an adult hold it high on the end of a broomstick. The children should take turns hitting the piñata with a plastic bat while blindfolded. Small children who are afraid of wearing a blindfold can just shut their eyes when it's their turn.

The piñata does not have to be broken to reveal its contents. If a child hits it just right, it will swing upside down, spilling everything.

EGG-CARTON TOY BIN

This project is made by hand and is very handy.

AGE GROUP

A lot of sewing is needed for this craft. It offers practice in eye-hand coordination as the child works to make his needle go where he wants it to go. This is a good craft for 4-, 5-, and 6-year-olds.

MATERIALS LIST

Each child needs:
◇ 7 Styrofoam egg cartons
◇ Scissors
◇ Yarn
◇ A plastic yarn needle (Sold wherever you can buy yarn.)
◇ A plastic bag (such as a carrying bag from a grocery store.)
◇ Stapler
◇ 1 or 2 permanent markers (not water-based)

DIRECTIONS

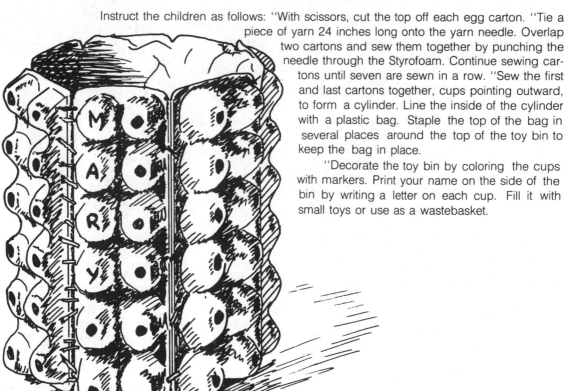

Instruct the children as follows: "With scissors, cut the top off each egg carton. "Tie a piece of yarn 24 inches long onto the yarn needle. Overlap two cartons and sew them together by punching the needle through the Styrofoam. Continue sewing cartons until seven are sewn in a row. "Sew the first and last cartons together, cups pointing outward, to form a cylinder. Line the inside of the cylinder with a plastic bag. Staple the top of the bag in several places around the top of the toy bin to keep the bag in place.

"Decorate the toy bin by coloring the cups with markers. Print your name on the side of the bin by writing a letter on each cup. Fill it with small toys or use as a wastebasket.

CYLINDER BEE

This is a wonderful, durable bee with a great big stinger that doesn't work.

AGE GROUP

All ages will like this craft. Preschoolers will learn to cut, glue, and assemble it. They can count six legs and learn the colors yellow and black. Children 7 years old and up will be more inventive. They will want to create their own version of the Cylinder Bee.

MATERIALS LIST

Each child needs:
◇ A toilet-paper roll
◇ Yellow, black, purple, and red construction paper
◇ A pencil
◇ A ruler
◇ Scissors
◇ Glue
◇ A paper fastener
◇ A 24″ piece of narrow crimped paper ribbon
◇ A paper punch
◇ Black and red markers

DIRECTIONS

Give the children the following directions: "Use a ruler and pencil to measure a rectangle 4½ × 6 inches onto yellow construction paper. Cut out the rectangle and spread glue on it. Wrap it around the toilet-paper roll, covering the roll completely.

"To make stripes on the bee, use the ruler and pencil to measure six black strips ½ × 5½ inches. Cut them out. Spread glue on three of the strips and wrap them around the cylinder.

"Use the other three strips to make legs. Put glue in the middle of each one. You can find the middle by folding the strip in half. Put glue on the fold. Stick the strips to the bottom of the Bee so they stick out straight at the sides. Bend each leg in half so it will stick out and then down.

"Use the pattern to trace wings onto purple construction paper. Cut out the wings. Glue the wings to the bee's back.

"Tie a 24-inch piece of ribbon to the top of a paper fastener. Force the fastener through the bee's back. Open the tabs inside the cylinder to keep the fastener in place.

"Use the pattern to trace two circles onto yellow construction paper. Cut them out. Apply glue to one end of the cylinder. Carefully press on a circle. Repeat with the other end of the bee.

"Use the paper punch to make eyes from black construction paper. Glue them to the bee's face. Use the black marker to add eyelashes and eyebrows. Use the red marker to draw a mouth.

"Use the pattern to trace a stinger onto red construction paper. Fold down the base of the stinger (as shown on the pattern). Put glue on the folded end and stick it to the end of the bee.

"Hang up your Cylinder Bee and let him dry before you play with him. Once he's dry, he can go sailing all over the place without falling apart."

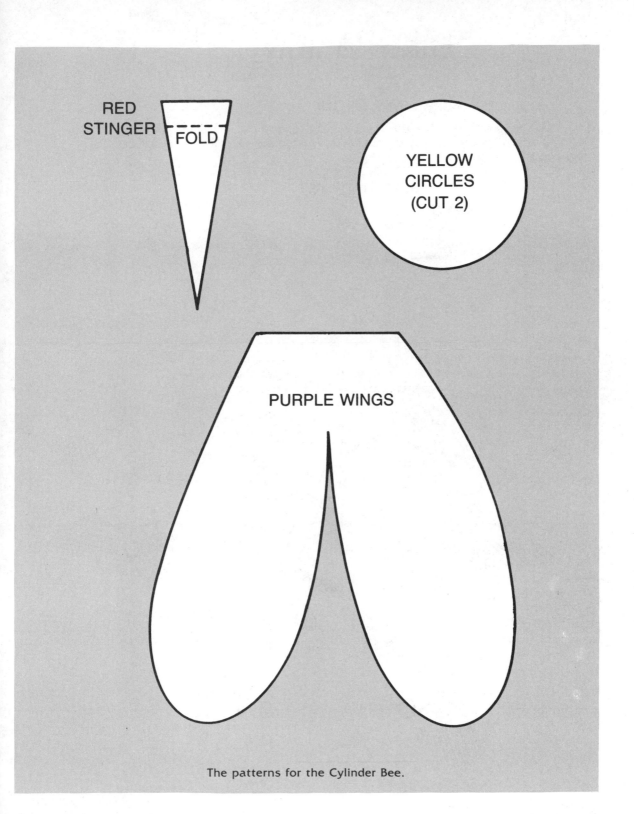

RED STINGER

FOLD

YELLOW CIRCLES (CUT 2)

PURPLE WINGS

The patterns for the Cylinder Bee.

CYLINDER BUTTERFLY

Its floppy wings flap when you lift it up and down.

AGE GROUP

All ages will enjoy this craft. Children 10 years old and younger can create their own wing colors and designs as they learn construction skills. Preschoolers will learn what a cylinder is and practice cutting, coloring, and gluing.

MATERIALS LIST

Each child needs:
◇ A toilet-paper roll
◇ A ruler
◇ A pencil
◇ Scissors
◇ Glue
◇ Crayons
◇ Markers
◇ Construction paper in many colors, including red and black
◇ A paper fastener
◇ A 24″ piece of narrow crimped paper ribbon
◇ A paper punch

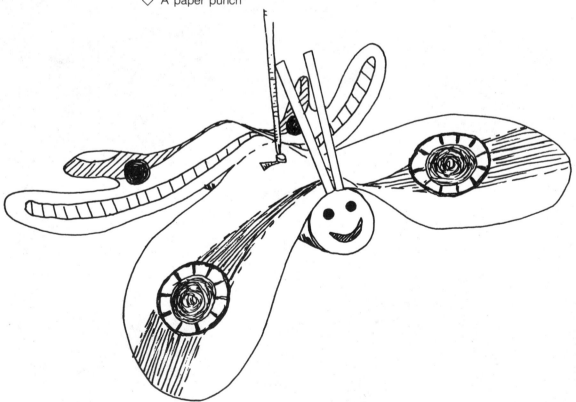

DIRECTIONS

Instruct the children as follows: "Use the ruler and pencil to draw a rectangle 4½ x 6 inches on construction paper. Cut out the rectangle and spread glue on it. Wrap the rectangle around the toilet-paper roll, covering the roll completely. This cylinder is the body of the butterfly.

"To make the wings, fold a piece of light-colored or white construction paper in half crosswise. Use the pattern to trace wings onto the paper, with the flat side of the pattern placed on the fold. Cut out through both papers, but do not cut the fold.

"Open the wings. Color on both sides with brightly colored markers and crayons. Glue the wings to the covered cylinder body.

"Insert a paper fastener through the back of the butterfly. Tie a 24-inch piece of ribbon to the top of the fastener. Spread out the tabs of the fastener inside the cylinder to hold the ribbon in place.

"Use the pattern to trace two circles onto construction paper. Cut out the circles. Make the face of the butterfly on one circle by gluing on a red paper mouth and two black eyes made with the paper punch. Spread glue on each end of the cylinder. Glue the face on the front of the butterfly, and the other circle on the back.

"Cut out two paper antennae ¼ x 4 inches. Glue them on the face. Make the butterfly's wings flap by gently liftly up and down on the ribbon."

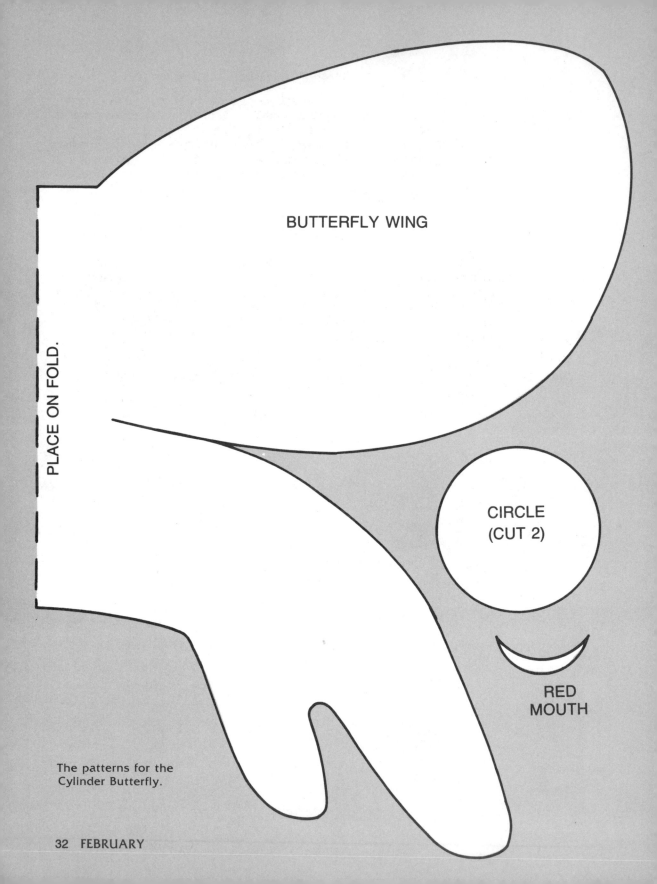

BUTTERFLY WING

PLACE ON FOLD.

CIRCLE
(CUT 2)

RED
MOUTH

The patterns for the
Cylinder Butterfly.

CYLINDER TRUCK

It could be a fire truck, or it could be loaded with dangerous chemicals! Whatever it is, the Cylinder Truck is easy to make and fun to play with.

AGE GROUP

This craft was designed for preschoolers from 2 to 6 years old. It lets children practice cutting, pasting, and drawing as they learn how to build a truck from a rectangle, a cylinder, and circles.

MATERIALS LIST

Each child needs:
◇ A pencil
◇ A ruler
◇ Scissors
◇ Glue
◇ Red, white, and black construction paper
◇ A toilet-paper roll
◇ Black marker
◇ White poster board for the wheels (Look in the School Supplies section of drugstores.)
◇ 4 paper fasteners

DIRECTIONS

Instruct the children as follows: "Use the pencil and ruler to measure a rectangle 4½ × 6 inches on red construction paper. Cut out the rectangle and apply glue to it. Wrap the rectangle around the toilet-paper roll, covering the roll completely.

"To make wheels, use the pattern to trace four circles onto the white poster board. Cut out the circles. Color around the edges of each circle with black marker to make them look like tires with whitewalls.

"Insert a paper fastener in the center of each wheel."

Use anything pointed to punch a small hole in each wheel so the child can insert the fastener. Then continue the instructions:

"Push the paper fasteners through the sides of the cylinder, two on one side and two on the other. Open the tabs to hold the wheels in place.

"Use the same pattern to draw two circles on red construction paper. Cut out the circles. Apply glue to the ends of the cylinder. Gently press a red circle on each end to seal them. Let them dry or they will try to pop off again.

"Measure a rectangle 1 × 1¼ inches on white construction paper. Draw a truck driver on the rectangle. Cut out the rectangle and glue it to the front of the truck.

"Use the pattern to draw a truck exhaust. It can also be a CB antenna. Glue it to the side of the truck so it sticks up near the front window. Your truck is ready to roll!"

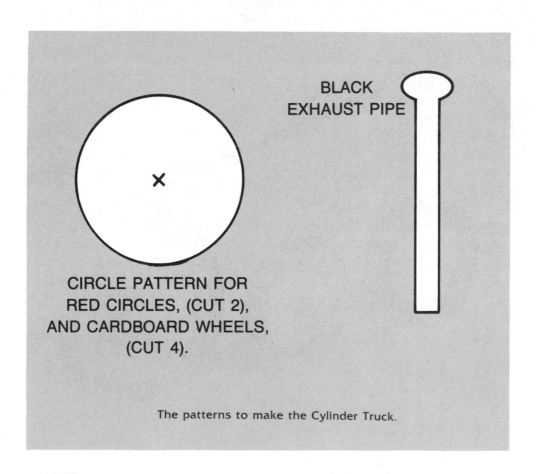

BLACK
EXHAUST PIPE

CIRCLE PATTERN FOR
RED CIRCLES, (CUT 2),
AND CARDBOARD WHEELS,
(CUT 4).

The patterns to make the Cylinder Truck.

DOILY BALLS

Use paper doilies to make these lovely and different decorations. Use them as snowballs to decorate a room. Fasten them to long pipe cleaners to make flowers. Add yarn for hair and glue on circle eyes to turn them into faces.

AGE GROUP

Children 7 years old and up enjoy making this craft. The children will learn to match doily patterns and to sew.

MATERIALS LIST

Each child needs:
◇ 12 to 24 round paper doilies (The doilies can be any size.)
◇ A needle threaded with double sewing thread, at least 2 feet long.
◇ Cellophane tape
◇ Scissors

DIRECTIONS

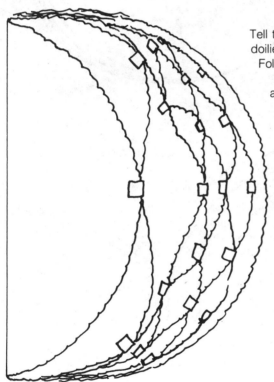

Tell the children the following directions: "Separate the paper doilies. Stack them on each other with their patterns matching. Fold each doily in half.

"With double sewing thread, stitch all 12 to 24 doilies at the fold to hold them together. First sew down, and then sew back up the fold to hold the doilies securely.

"Tape two doilies together at a place where their patterns match. Next tape two more doilies together at the same place on the pattern. Continue taping the doilies in the same design spot all around the ball.

"Tape two different doilies together at a different spot on the design. Continue around the doily ball, taping two doilies at a time on this second design spot.

"The doilies can be taped in three or more different places all around the doily ball. Be sure the doily designs match, and be sure you are taping at the same place on each doily. The doily ball will open up in a honeycomb pattern, similar to paper ornaments found in card shops.

How to fasten the Doily Ball with tape.

Three steps to make the Doily Ball.

1.

2.

3.

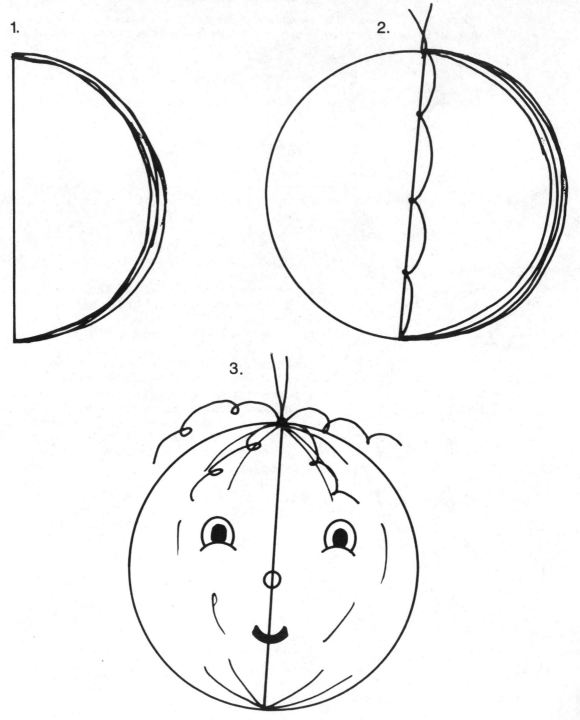

MUFFIN-CUP FLOWERS

Preschoolers practice printing their names, cutting, gluing, and drawing while making these posies.

AGE GROUP

This craft was especially designed for children ages 2 to 6.

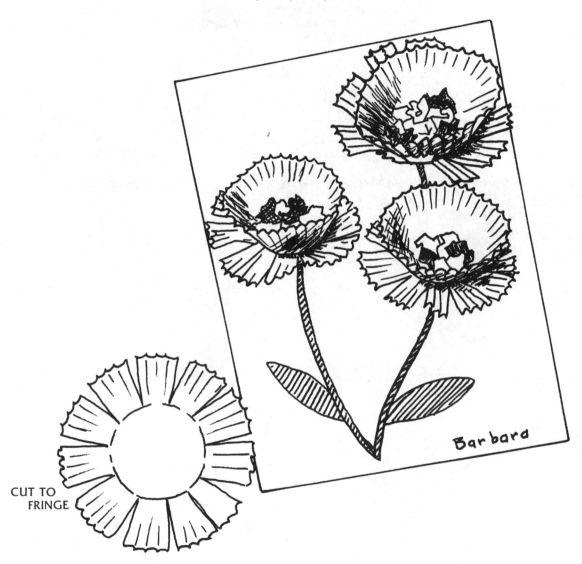

CUT TO
FRINGE

Barbara

MATERIALS LIST

Each child needs:
◇ Construction paper
◇ Scissors
◇ Glue
◇ Paper bake cups (Muffin-cup liners)
◇ A green marker
◇ Tissue wrapping paper in several colors,
   cut into 1½" squares (Found in the Card
   section of drugstores.)

DIRECTIONS

Instruct the children as follows: "Fringe three muffin cups by cutting all around the edges toward the center. Spread glue on the bottoms of the fringed cups and press them onto a sheet of construction paper.

"Glue a whole muffin cup in the center of each fringed one. Then spread glue in the center of each whole cup. Crumple a few pieces of colored wrapping paper and press them into the cups.

"Use a green marker to draw stems and leaves for the flowers. Print your name on your flower garden."

TORTILLA PIZZA

This snack is nutritious and very delicious.

MATERIALS LIST

Each child needs:
◇ 1 small flour tortilla
◇ 1 tablespoon spaghetti sauce
◇ 2 tablespoons shredded cheddar cheese
◇ 3 slices pepperoni
◇ Parmesan cheese
◇ A pie pan or paper plate

DIRECTIONS

Tell the children to lay the tortillas on a pie pan for heating in the oven, or lay them on paper plates for heating in the microwave. Then have them spread spaghetti sauce on the tortilla and sprinkle it with shredded cheese. Tell them to add the pepperoni slices and sift on some parmesan cheese.

Broil each tortilla pizza in the oven about 2 minutes, or until the cheese melts. You also can microwave on high for ½ minute. The children can eat it as is, or fold it in half to eat.

CARROT COOKIES

What a way to get vitamin A into your day! These cookies are so loaded with carrots you could almost serve them with pot roast.

MATERIALS LIST

◇ A large bowl
◇ A wooden spoon
◇ Solid shortening
◇ A cookie sheet
◇ ¾ cup soft margarine (1½ sticks)
◇ 1 cup brown sugar, firmly packed
◇ 1 egg
◇ ¼ cup milk
◇ 1 teaspoon orange extract
◇ 2¼ cups grated raw carrot
◇ 2¼ cups flour
◇ 1 cup dry oatmeal
◇ 2 teaspoons baking powder
◇ ½ teaspoon salt
◇ ¾ cup raisins

DIRECTIONS

The children can grease the cookie sheet, using solid shortening and their fingers. Help them measure the margarine, firmly packed brown sugar, and egg into the large bowl. Let them take turns stirring the mixture until it is well mixed and fluffy.

The children should stir in the milk and orange extract. Then they should add the grated carrot and stir the batter well.

Help them measure the flour, oatmeal, baking powder, and salt, and add these ingredients to the cookie dough. Last of all, they can measure and stir in the raisins.

Show the children how to drop a teaspoonful of dough onto the greased cookie sheet. Space the cookies a little apart. Bake them in a preheated oven at 350° F for 15 minutes, until light brown around the edges. Store them in a tightly covered container. You can freeze them.

This recipe makes 3 dozen cookies.

MARCH
CRAFTS

March crafts include several Wind Friends that prevent boredom by encouraging physical activity. Who can make one of these brightly colored, streamer-laden creations without twirling it about the head, running, jumping, and dancing to watch it swirl around?

March can come in like a lion and go out like a lamb, again with the help of toilet-roll cylinders. My family uses such a large amount of toilet paper that I had to think up something to do with all those empty rolls.

MARCH LION

He has two legs that look like four, and a muffin-cup mane. Let the March winds roar!

AGE GROUP

This is a good craft for children 5 years old and up.

MATERIALS LIST

Each child needs:
◇ A toilet-paper roll
◇ A pencil
◇ A ruler
◇ Yellow, brown, black, and red construction paper
◇ Scissors
◇ Glue
◇ A paper muffin-cup liner
◇ A paper punch
◇ Black pen

DIRECTIONS

Instruct the children as follows: "Cut an end off the toilet-paper roll so the roll is 3 inches long.

"Use the pencil and ruler to measure a rectangle 3 × 6 inches on yellow construction paper. Cut out the rectangle. Draw two smaller rectangles 2½ × 4½ inches on yellow paper and cut them out.

"Use the pattern to trace and cut out two large yellow circles, two small brown circles, two yellow ears, and a brown tail. Fringe the tail (as shown on the pattern). Spread glue on the large yellow rectangle. Wrap it around the toilet-paper roll to cover it.

"Roll each of the smaller rectangles into cylinders 2½ inches long. Overlap the edges a little and glue them to make them hold their shape. Draw four 1½-inch slits down one end of each cylinder; space them equally apart. Cut the slits. Spread them out to form four tabs on each cylinder.

"To make the front feet, cut one tab off one cylinder. Apply glue to the three remaining tabs. Glue the cylinder on the bottom of the lion so that two tabs wrap around the lion's sides, and the third tab stretches back along its stomach. Press on the tabs until they stay in place. Use a black pen to draw a line straight down the middle of the foot, dividing it into what looks like two feet.

"To make the back feet, cut two tabs off the remaining cylinder (as shown). Put glue on the two tabs that are left. Glue the cylinder to the bottom of the lion, behind the front foot, so the tabs wrap around the lion's sides. Press on the tabs until they stick in place. Again use a black marker to divide this foot with a line, making it look like two feet.

"Apply glue to the back end of the toilet-paper roll, around the edge. Gently press a yellow circle onto the glue to make a behind for the lion. Glue on the tail.

"Apply glue to the front of the toilet-paper roll, around the edge. Gently press on a muffin-cup liner. Snip the liner all around with scissors to make it stand out more.

"Put glue on the remaining yellow circle. Glue the circle in the center of the muffin-cup mane. Glue on the ears (as shown).

"Add two brown-circle cheeks. Draw three dots on each. Add two black eyes, a black nose, and a red mouth made with the paper punch."

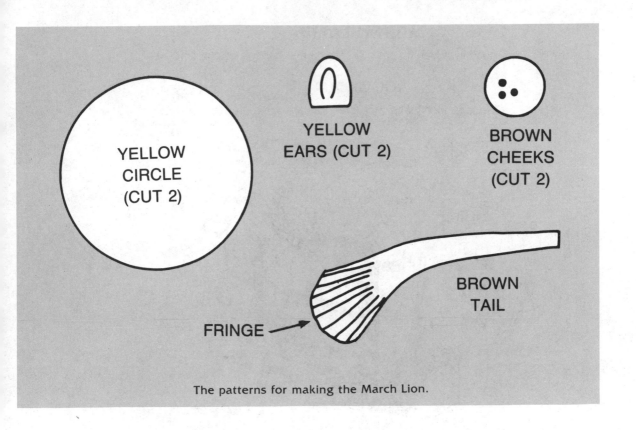

YELLOW
CIRCLE
(CUT 2)

YELLOW
EARS (CUT 2)

BROWN
CHEEKS
(CUT 2)

BROWN
TAIL

FRINGE

The patterns for making the March Lion.

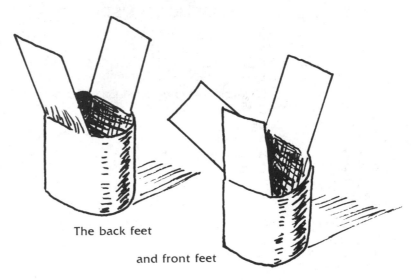

The back feet

and front feet

of the March Lion and March Lamb.

MARCH LAMB

Let the March winds blow! March Lamb will be warm in her soft coat of cotton balls.

AGE GROUP

This is a good craft for children 5 years old and up.

MATERIALS LIST

Each child needs:
◇ A toilet-paper roll
◇ A pencil
◇ A ruler
◇ White, black, and pink construction paper
◇ Scissors
◇ Glue
◇ A paper punch
◇ A black pen
◇ Cotton balls

DIRECTIONS

Give the children the following directions: "Cut an end off the toilet-paper roll so the roll is 3 inches long.

"Use a pencil and ruler to measure a rectangle 3 x 5½ inches on white construction paper. Cut out the rectangle. Draw two smaller rectangles 2½ x 4½ inches on white paper and cut them out.

"Use the pattern to trace and cut out two large white circles, a small pink circle, and three white shapes for the ears and tail. Spread glue on the large white rectangle. Wrap it around the toilet-paper roll to cover it.

"Roll each of the smaller rectangles into cylinders 2½ inches long. Overlap the edges a little and glue to make them hold their shape. Draw four 1½-inch slits down one end of each cylinder. Space them equally apart. Cut the slits. Spread them out to form four tabs on each cylinder.

"To make the front feet, cut one tab off one cylinder. Spread glue on the remaining three tabs. Glue the cylinder on the bottom of the lamb so that two tabs wrap around the lamb's sides, and the third tab stretches back across its stomach. Press on the tabs until they stay in place. Use a black pen to draw a line straight down the middle of this foot, dividing it into what looks like two feet.

"To make the back feet, cut two tabs that are opposite one another off the remaining cylinder (as shown for the March Lion). Put glue on the two tabs that are left. Glue the cylinder to the bottom of the lamb, behind the front foot, so that the tabs wrap around the lamb's sides. Press on the tabs until they stick in place. Again use a black pen to visually divide this foot with a line, making it look like two feet.

"Apply glue to the end of the toilet-paper roll that is nearest the back feet. Gently press a white circle onto the glue, closing the roll and making a behind for the lamb.

"Apply glue to the front end of the toilet-paper roll, around the edge. Gently press on the remaining white circle.

"Hold the lamb by her legs and spread glue all over the body. Snip cotton balls with scissors and cover the body with tufts of cotton.

"Glue a thin layer of cotton to the lamb's face. Glue a pink circle in the middle of the lamb's face. Add two black eyes and a white nose made with the paper punch. Use a black pen to draw a tiny mouth. Glue an ear on each side of the lamb's face. Glue the tail on the back, hanging down."

WOOLIE-PULLIE

The children can use milk bottle caps for easy one-finger gluing. Give each child a cap, squirt in some white glue, and show them how to use one finger to spread the glue on their craft. If someone is squeamish and doesn't want to use a finger, he can dip in a toothpick or popsicle stick to spread the glue. At the end of craft time, throw the cap away.

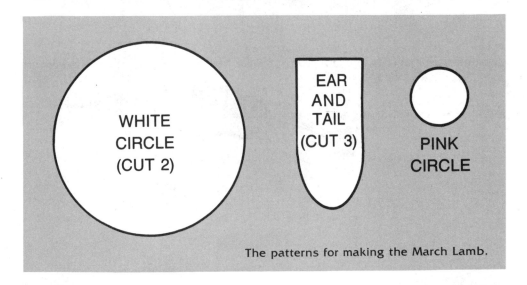

WHITE CIRCLE (CUT 2)

EAR AND TAIL (CUT 3)

PINK CIRCLE

The patterns for making the March Lamb.

LEPRECHAUN HAT

The leprechaun, a tiny elf from Irish folklore, will come alive before your eyes when your wee one wears this hat.

AGE GROUP

. This craft was designed for children from age 2 to age 6 to make on St. Patrick's Day, March 17.

MATERIALS LIST

Each child needs:
◇ A pencil
◇ A ruler
◇ Scissors
◇ Glue
◇ Brown, green, and black construction paper
◇ Stapler (optional)

DIRECTIONS

Tell the children the following instructions: "Fold a sheet of brown construction paper in half crosswise. Place the hat pattern on the fold. Trace around the pattern. Cut out, being careful not to cut on the fold. Open out to a full-sized hat.

"Do the same with the patterns for the hat band and the shamrock. Fold black construction paper in half. Place the hat-band pattern on the fold. Trace around it and cut it out. Fold the green construction paper in half. Place the shamrock pattern on the fold. Trace around it and cut out.

"Use the pencil and ruler to measure two brown paper strips 1½ × 11 inches each. Now the hat is ready to assemble.

"Glue the hatband on the hat. Glue the shamrock in the middle of the band. Glue or staple the two paper strips behind the brim of the hat."

Fit the hat on the front of the child's head. Overlap the edges of the paper strips behind his head. Glue or staple the overlapped edges so the hat will fit.

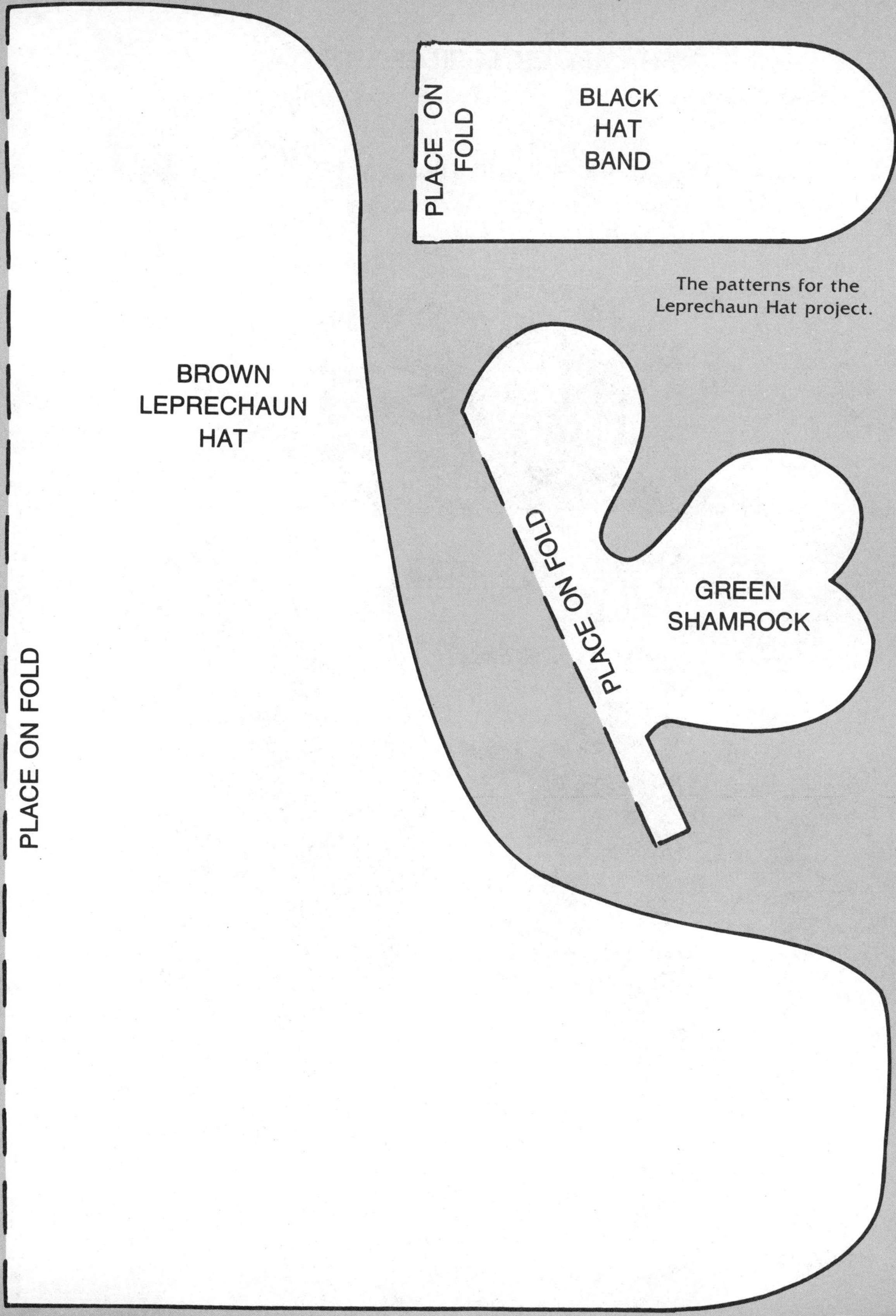

PLACE ON FOLD

BLACK
HAT
BAND

The patterns for the
Leprechaun Hat project.

BROWN
LEPRECHAUN
HAT

PLACE ON FOLD

PLACE ON FOLD

GREEN
SHAMROCK

SHAMROCK LEPRECHAUN

The national emblem of Ireland, the shamrock, is used as the body and head of this elf. Make him on March 17, Saint Patrick's Day!

AGE GROUP

This craft will challenge children 7 years old and up.

MATERIALS LIST

Each child needs:

◇ A pencil
◇ A ruler
◇ Scissors
◇ Glue
◇ Green, black, white, and red construction paper
◇ A black marker

DIRECTIONS

The children should begin by making the arms and legs. They can set them aside to dry while putting the body together. Making the arms and legs is a little complex, but it's a nice construction technique for them to learn. Instruct the children as follows:

"Use the pencil and ruler to measure eight strips of green construction paper, 1 × 12 inches each. To make one arm, lay two strips at right angles to each other, one on top of the other, forming the letter L. Fold the bottom strip over the top strip and press with your fingers. Repeat, folding the strips upon each other until they are completely folded. Glue the ends to keep them from unfolding. Repeat this process three more times with the remaining strips. You will then have two arms and two legs. Set them aside.

"Use the pattern to trace a shamrock onto green construction paper that has been folded in half crosswise. Lay the flat side of the shamrock pattern on the fold. Trace around the pattern. Cut out through both papers, but do not cut the folded edge. Open into a whole shamrock.

"Fold a sheet of black construction paper in half crosswise. Lay the hat pattern on the fold. Trace around it. Cut out through both papers, once again being careful not to cut the fold. Open to a whole hat.

"Use the patterns to trace two vests, two eyeballs, and a bow tie onto black construction paper. Trace two eyes and a vest onto white paper. Cut out all these pieces.

"Put Shamrock Leprechaun together by gluing the hat on the top of the shamrock. Glue on the white eyes, black eyeballs, and red mouth.

"Draw wiggly lines down the vest to look like ruffles. Glue the vest below the mouth. Glue a jacket piece on each side of the vest, covering it slightly. (The front edge of the vest is marked on the pattern.) Add the black bow tie at the top of the vest. Glue the arms and legs on the front of the leprechaun.

"Hang Shamrock Leprechaun up with tape, or lean him against something on a table."

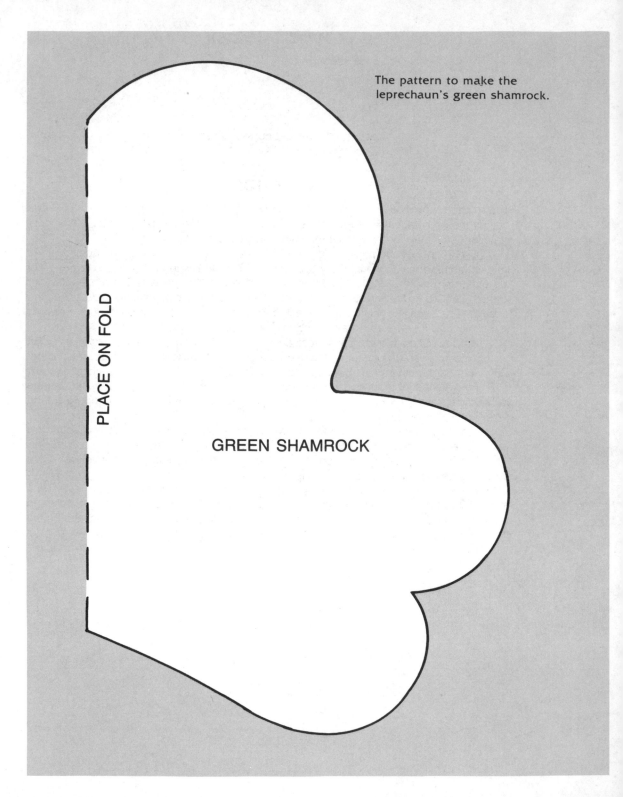

The pattern to make the leprechaun's green shamrock.

PLACE ON FOLD

GREEN SHAMROCK

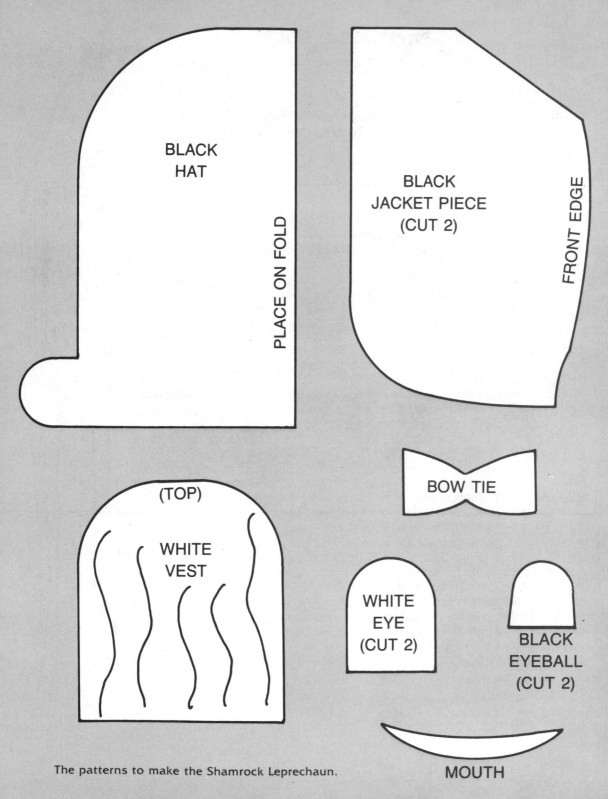

BLACK
HAT

PLACE ON FOLD

BLACK
JACKET PIECE
(CUT 2)

FRONT EDGE

(TOP)

WHITE
VEST

BOW TIE

WHITE
EYE
(CUT 2)

BLACK
EYEBALL
(CUT 2)

MOUTH

The patterns to make the Shamrock Leprechaun.

PAPER WIND SOCK

This is a beautiful way to catch the breeze. Twirl the wind sock or hang it.

AGE GROUP

This wind sock is an ideal craft for all children, beginning at age 2. Very young creators can decorate the wind sock; an adult can assemble it with a little "help" from the child. Older children can glue and tie the wind sock themselves.

MATERIALS LIST

Each child needs:
◇ A 9" × 12" sheet of white construction paper
◇ Water-based markers and/or crayons
◇ Crepe-paper streamers (Look in the Party section of grocery and drug stores.)
◇ Narrow crimped paper ribbon, cut into three 10" pieces and one 24" piece
◇ A paper punch
◇ A stapler
◇ Cellophane tape

DIRECTIONS

Instruct the children as follows: "Color a bright design on one side of the white paper. The brighter the colors, the prettier the wind sock will be.

"Hold the paper so the long sides are at the top and bottom. Fold the top down 1 inch. Roll the paper into a cylinder 9 inches long with the folded edge on the inside and the colored design on the outside. Glue it to make it hold its shape.

"Cut a 12-inch crepe-paper streamer. Staple it around the bottom edge of the cylinder. Cut four crepe-paper streamers, each 24 inches long. Staple one end of each streamer inside the bottom edge of the cylinder so the streamers hang down.

"Use the paper punch to make three holes an equal distance apart around the top edge of the cylinder. Tie one end of a ribbon in each hole. Tie the ends of these three ribbons together to make a single knot. Tie the 24-inch ribbon below this knot.

"Twirl the wind sock around or hang it up to catch the breeze."

Wind socks can be made with sheets of 12- × -18-inch construction paper, following the method just given. They can fit any season of the year, depending on the colors chosen for their construction. For Halloween, make Pumpkin Wind Socks from orange paper and green streamers. Glue black triangle eyes and nose and a black paper mouth on the side of the craft. Make a Ghost Wind Sock with white paper and white streamers. Add black circle eyes and nose, and a black mouth.

HAPPY BIRTHDAY WIND FRIEND

This easy-to-make toy is a good party favor. Make one for each guest ahead of time or help the children make their own for a crafty birthday theme. The children can use them to dance and keep time to music.

AGE GROUP

This craft was designed especially for children from age 2 to 7, but I have caught my 10-year-old playing with it, too.

MATERIALS LIST

Each child needs:
◇ A pencil
◇ A ruler
◇ Scissors
◇ Glue
◇ A toilet-paper roll
◇ A paper punch
◇ Brightly colored birthday wrapping paper
◇ Narrow crimped paper ribbon
◇ Streamers (Look in the Party section of grocery and drug stores.)

DIRECTIONS

Give the children the following instructions: ''Use the pencil and ruler to draw a rectangle 4½ × 5½ inches on the birthday wrapping paper. Cut out the rectangle. Spread glue on the paper. Wrap it around the toilet-paper roll, covering the roll completely.

''Use the paper punch to make three holes, evenly spaced, around each end of the covered roll. The holes should be made ¼ inch from the edge.

''Cut three pieces of crimped ribbon 10 inches long each. Tie a ribbon in each hole at one end of the covered roll. Tie these ribbons together at the top. Tie a 24-inch piece of ribbon to this knot.

''Cut three paper streamers 24 inches long each. Twist one end of a streamer so it can be inserted in a hole at the other end of the paper roll. Push the streamer through a hole and tie it in a knot to keep it in place. If you tie the knot inside the paper roll, it will look neater. Trim the end of the knot. Repeat with the other two streamers.''

PAPER-PLATE WIND FRIEND

Use bright markers to draw a friendly face. Add ribbon and streamers and let your new friend sail in the wind.

AGE GROUP

Children from ages 2 to 7 will enjoy this craft. They practice drawing a face, printing their names, and tying knots.

MATERIALS LIST

Each child needs:
◇ A 9″ white paper plate (Generic plates work best.)
◇ Water-based markers
◇ A paper punch
◇ Narrow crimped paper ribbon
◇ Streamers (Look in the Party section of grocery and drug stores.)
◇ Scissors

DIRECTIONS

Give the children the following instructions: ''Use markers to draw a bright, happy face on the paper plate. Draw a big bow under the mouth. Print your name across the top of the face.

''Use the paper punch to make four holes ¼ inch from the edge of the plate. Punch one hole at the top of the plate, one at the bottom, and one on each side.

''Measure four pieces of crimped ribbon, 14 inches long each. Tie an end of one ribbon through a hole with a tight knot. Repeat with the remaining ribbons, tying one ribbon per hole. Tie the ends of the four ribbons together above the wind friend's face. Tie an 18-inch piece of ribbon to this knot.

''Cut four paper streamers 30 inches long each. Twist one end of a streamer so it can be inserted through a hole in the wind friend. Push the streamer through one of the four holes, pull it through a little, and tie it in a knot to hold it in place. Repeat with the other three streamers. Trim the end of the knots.

''Grab your wind friend by its ribbon and sail it around the yard.''

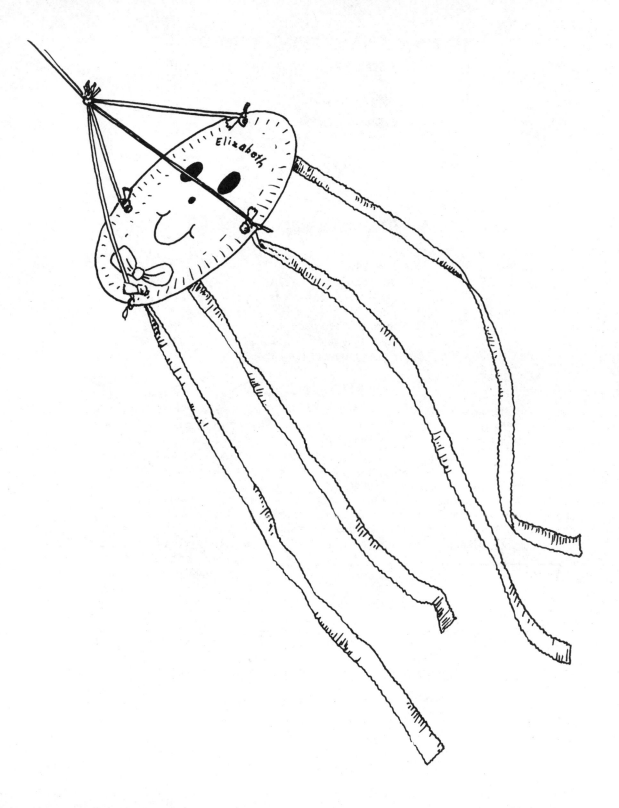

THAT'S-MY-NAME WIND FRIEND

Dance with the breeze and take your own wind friend along.

AGE GROUP

Children from ages 2 to 7 practice cutting, tying knots, and printing their name while making this craft.

MATERIALS LIST

Each child needs:

◇ A pencil
◇ A ruler
◇ Scissors
◇ Glue
◇ Construction paper
◇ A paper punch
◇ A stapler
◇ A marker
◇ Narrow crimped paper ribbon
◇ Streamers (In the Party section
  of most grocery or drug stores.)

DIRECTIONS

Instruct the children as follows: "Use the pencil and ruler to draw a rectangle 4½ × 9 inches on construction paper. Cut out the rectangle. Fold the paper in half lengthwise to make a rectangle 9 inches long. Hold it so the fold is at the top.

"Cut four paper streamers 30 inches long each. Open the rectangle and lay the streamers on it so they are flat and evenly spaced. Staple them to the underside of the rectangle. Glue the rectangle closed, sealing the streamers inside.

"Use the paper punch to make three holes close to the top edge of the rectangle and spaced evenly apart. Tie one end of a 10-inch crimped paper ribbon in each hole. Tie the other ends of these ribbons together with a knot. Tie an 18-inch piece of ribbon to this knot.

"Print your name on the rectangle in big letters with a marker. Hold your wind friend by its ribbon and twirl it around your head. Hang it in your room to catch the breeze."

How to staple That's-My-Name Wind Friend.

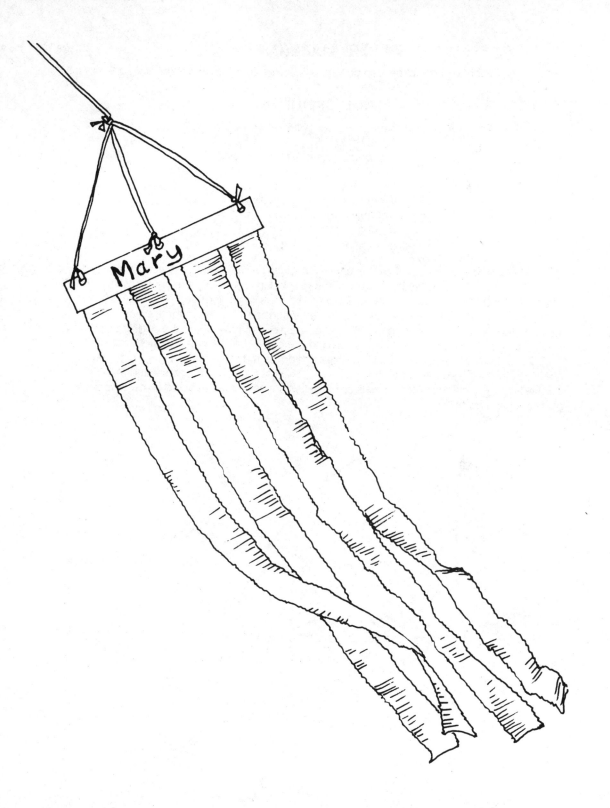

PAPER AIRPLANE

A sheet of typing or notebook paper can be turned into a circle that soars with the flip of a wrist.

AGE GROUP

This is a quick and easy craft for children 8 years old and up.

MATERIALS LIST

Each child needs:
◇ A sheet of typing or notebook paper
◇ Cellophane tape (optional)

DIRECTIONS

Instruct the children as follows: "Fold the paper into a triangle with the two tips even and about 1⅛ inches apart. Fold up the bottom of the triangle ¾ inch, pressing the fold flat with your fingers. Fold the bottom up ¾ inch again, pressing it well with your fingers.

"Curl it into a circle with the folded collar on the inside. One end of the collar will slip into the other end, closing the circle. You can add a piece of tape where the ends come together, but it is not necessary. Pinch all around the collar until it forms a perfect circle.

"To fly this airplane, grasp it with two fingers inside, on top of the triangle tips. Your thumb goes on the outside, under your fingers. Cock your wrist back and flip your hand forward, quickly letting go of the airplane. It flies collar-first with amazing ease, doing its own version of dips, spins, and twirls."

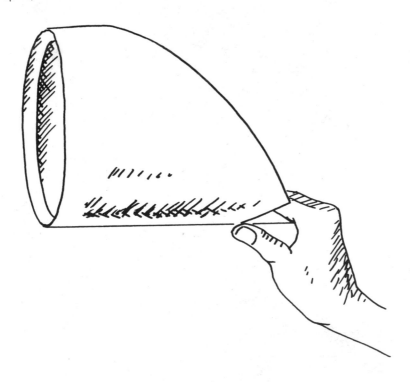

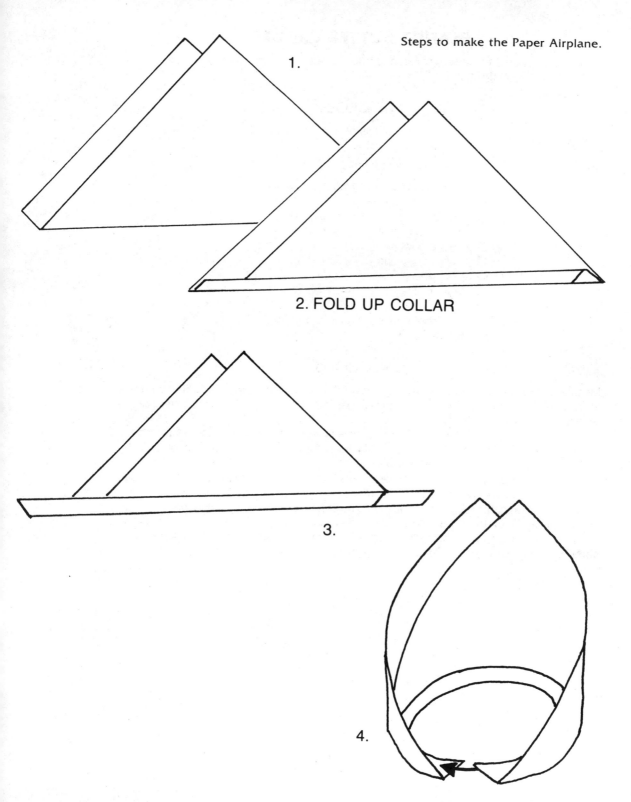

Steps to make the Paper Airplane.

1.

2. FOLD UP COLLAR

3.

4.

Paper Airplane 59

PEANUT BUTTER CREMES

This is a delicious way to teach children to follow directions, to measure, and to stay with a project until it is completed.

AGE GROUP

Any child can make this dessert with a little help.

MATERIALS LIST

◇ A 6-ounce package (1 cup) chocolate chips
◇ 1 cup peanut butter
◇ ½ cup sweetened condensed milk
◇ ¼ cup confectioners' sugar
◇ A large bowl
◇ A wooden spoon
◇ Wax paper
◇ Paper plates
◇ Pencils
◇ Extra confectioners' sugar in a bowl
◇ A fork

DIRECTIONS

Melt the chocolate chips in a double boiler over hot water. Stir until smooth. If you have a microwave oven, pour the chocolate chips into a large microwave bowl. Cover and microwave on high for 3 minutes. Remove from the oven. Stir until smooth.

Help the children add the peanut butter, sweetened condensed milk, and confectioners' sugar to the melted chocolate. They can take turns stirring with a wooden spoon until the mixture gets stiff. This takes 2 or 3 minutes.

Give everyone a paper plate and a pencil. Each child should write his name on the plate. Lay a piece of wax paper over the name. Divide the creme mixture among the children.

The children can roll pieces of dough into balls the size of a large marble, and put them on their plates. Show them how to dip a fork in powdered sugar and press each ball to flatten it slightly. Refrigerate the Peanut Butter Cremes until firm, about 30 minutes. This recipe makes about 55 1-inch Cremes if no one eats them before you count.

APRIL
CRAFTS

This chapter is filled with ideas for creating chicks, making things with eggs and eggshells, and decorating baskets as the children's thoughts turn to Easter. There's even a recipe for baking cookies using a discarded chocolate bunny.

NICKNACK CHICK

Don't throw away the empty eggshells and old milk lids! Children can turn them into a Nicknack Chick for a pleasing table decoration.

AGE GROUP

Children from ages 2 to 10 will enjoy making groups of these economic chicks. It's fun to make a cute little something from nothing.

MATERIALS LIST

◇ Several empty eggshell halves, washed and allowed to dry
◇ Plastic lids from gallon milk bottles
◇ Colorful markers
◇ Tissue wrapping paper, any color
◇ Large cotton balls
◇ Black and orange construction paper
◇ Scissors
◇ Glue
◇ A paper punch

DIRECTIONS

Instruct the children as follows: "Color the outside of the eggshells with colorful markers. Handle the shell carefully."

If a shell breaks, just throw it away and let the child color another one. Then tell them:

"Cut out a tissue-paper circle (using the pattern). Crumple this circle by squeezing it in your hand. Spread glue inside the eggshell. Then unfold the crumpled circle and line the inside of the egg with it.

"Use the remaining patterns to draw orange feet and an orange diamond beak. Cut them out. Fold the beak in half.

"Make black eyes with black paper and the paper punch. Squirt a generous amount of glue into the plastic milk lid. Glue the eyes, beak, and feet onto a cotton-ball chick by dipping each piece into the glue, then applying it to the chick.

"Dip the finished chick into the glue and set it inside the lined shell. Then set the shell in the milk lid full of glue. Let Nicknack Chick dry overnight."

The children can make several of these chicks and set them around in groups of two or three.

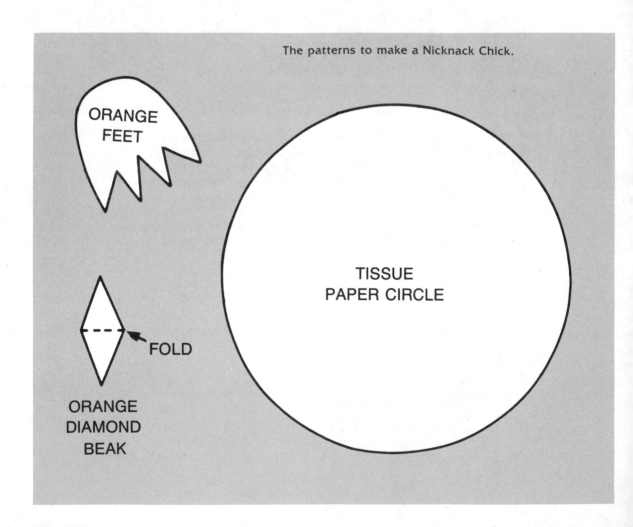

The patterns to make a Nicknack Chick.

ORANGE FEET

FOLD

ORANGE DIAMOND BEAK

TISSUE PAPER CIRCLE

BE-A-BUNNY

Let your little ones dress up as Be-A-Bunny for some Easter fun.

AGE GROUP

This craft is designed for children from ages 2 to 6. Encourage children age 4 and up to cut, color, and glue the ears.

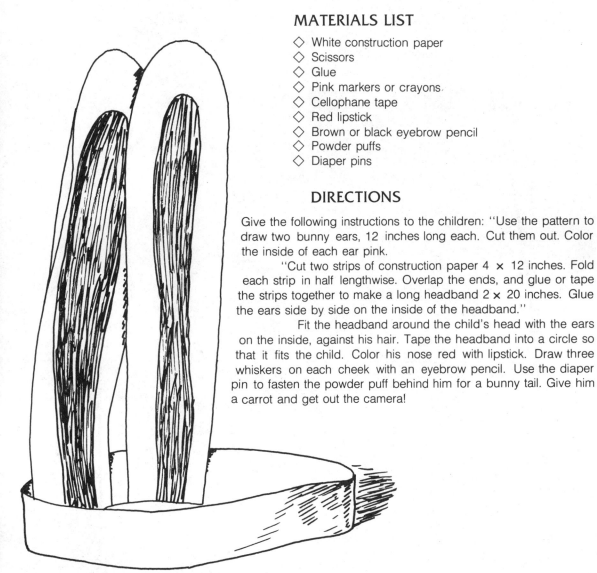

MATERIALS LIST

◇ White construction paper
◇ Scissors
◇ Glue
◇ Pink markers or crayons
◇ Cellophane tape
◇ Red lipstick
◇ Brown or black eyebrow pencil
◇ Powder puffs
◇ Diaper pins

DIRECTIONS

Give the following instructions to the children: "Use the pattern to draw two bunny ears, 12 inches long each. Cut them out. Color the inside of each ear pink.

"Cut two strips of construction paper 4 x 12 inches. Fold each strip in half lengthwise. Overlap the ends, and glue or tape the strips together to make a long headband 2 x 20 inches. Glue the ears side by side on the inside of the headband."

Fit the headband around the child's head with the ears on the inside, against his hair. Tape the headband into a circle so that it fits the child. Color his nose red with lipstick. Draw three whiskers on each cheek with an eyebrow pencil. Use the diaper pin to fasten the powder puff behind him for a bunny tail. Give him a carrot and get out the camera!

The ear pattern for Be-A-Bunny.

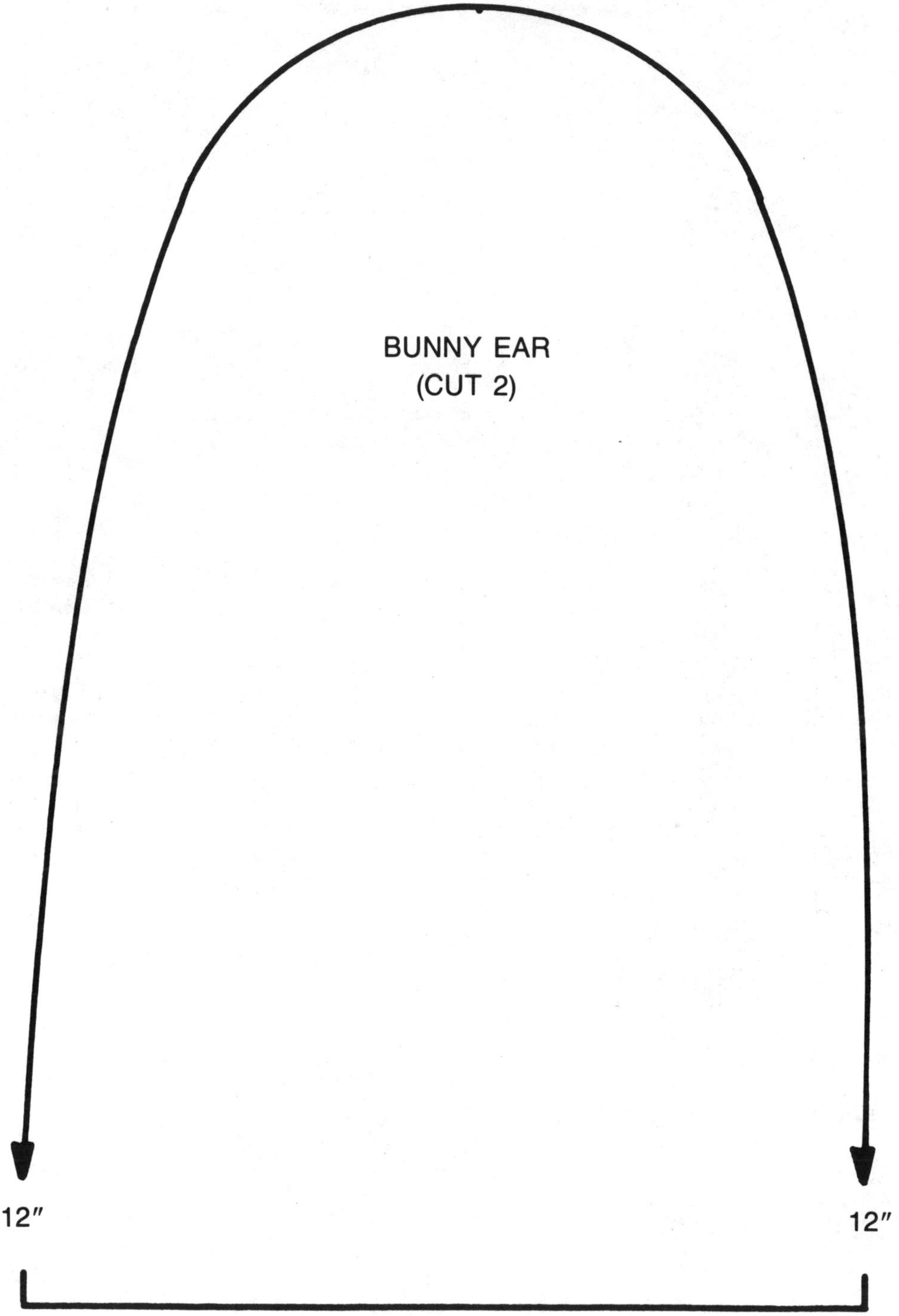

BUNNY EAR
(CUT 2)

12"   12"

POP-UP EGG

The chick comes out to wish everyone a Happy Easter. Make this card to keep or to give away.

AGE GROUP

This is a good craft for all ages. Preschoolers will practice cutting, gluing, and writing skills while working with the circle and diamond shapes.

MATERIALS LIST

Each child needs:
◇ A pencil
◇ A black marker
◇ Scissors
◇ Glue
◇ Construction paper in many colors, including yellow
◇ Sequins, glitter, paper scraps, cloth scraps (optional)

DIRECTIONS

Instruct the children as follows: "To make the egg, fold a sheet of construction paper in half crosswise. Place the bottom of the egg pattern on the fold. Trace around it. Cut out through both papers, but do not cut the fold.

"Cut a 3½-inch slot in the top egg only (as shown on the pattern). This is the slot the chick goes into. Glue the two papers together by spreading a thin line of glue around the edge of the egg."

This "glue line" is shown on the egg pattern. Help small children with this step to prevent them from gluing the slot closed. Then tell the children:

"Use the patterns to trace a chick onto yellow paper and a diamond-shaped beak onto orange paper. Cut the pieces out. Fold the beak in half (as shown on the pattern). Glue it on the chick's face.

"Draw black circle eyes with a marker. Write a message on the chick, such as: *HAPPY EASTER!* or *HAPPY SPRING!*

"Decorate the egg by gluing on paper circles and stripes of pretty colors. You can also decorate with sequins, cloth scraps, glitter, tissue paper, or pieces of paper doilies to make a very fancy egg.

"Print your name on the front of the Pop-Up Egg. Slide the chick into the slot so only his head is showing. Give it to someone you love."

The patterns for the Pop-Up Egg project.

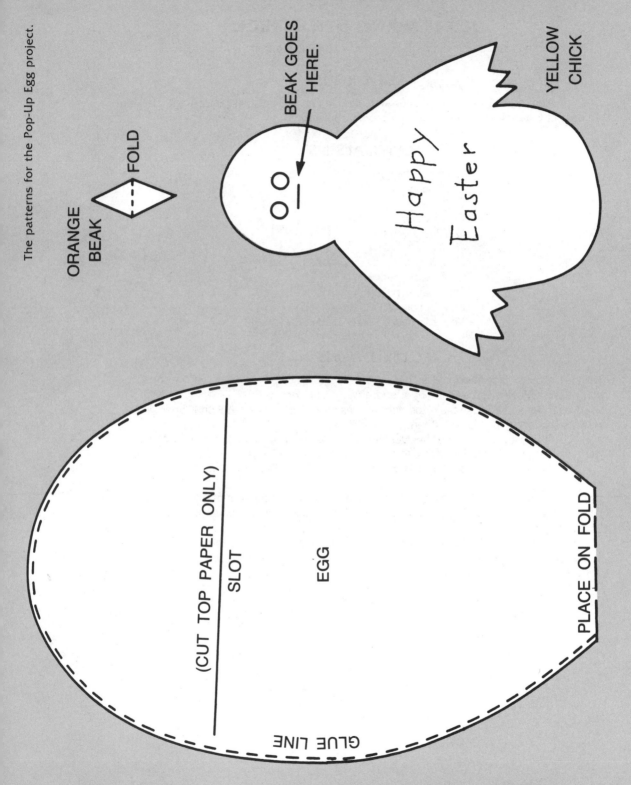

ORANGE BEAK

FOLD

BEAK GOES HERE.

O O

YELLOW CHICK

Happy Easter

(CUT TOP PAPER ONLY)

SLOT

EGG

GLUE LINE

PLACE ON FOLD

OLD HEN AND LITTLE CHICK

Which came first, the chicken or the egg? You can include both in this whimsical craft.

AGE GROUP

Children from ages 2 to 7 will have fun with Old Hen and Little Chick. Encourage children 4 years old and older to cut out the pieces themselves.

MATERIALS LIST

For each child you need:
◇ A pencil
◇ A ruler
◇ Scissors
◇ Glue
◇ Crayons
◇ Yellow and black construction paper
◇ A black marker
◇ A paper punch
◇ A cotton ball
You also need a razor blade

DIRECTIONS

Tell the children the following: "Use the patterns to trace the following onto yellow construction paper: Old Hen, a beak, an egg, and a wing. Cut them out."

For Adults Only: Use the razor blade to make two ¾-inch slits, 1½ inches apart, in Old Hen as shown on the pattern. Then tell the children:

"Use the black marker to draw Old Hen's face (as shown). Color the comb and wattle with crayons. Add some feathers with crayons, too.

"Fold down the flap on the wing. Put glue on the flap. Glue the wings above the slits in the body.

"Glue a cotton-ball chick below the slits in the body. Use the paper punch to make two black circle eyes for Little Chick. Fold the beak in half (as shown on the pattern). Glue it below Little Chick's eyes.

"Insert the long tab of the egg through the two slits. Pull the tab to the right so the egg is hidden behind Old Hen. Push the tab to the left so Old Hen can lay the egg. The chick will stay warm under her wing."

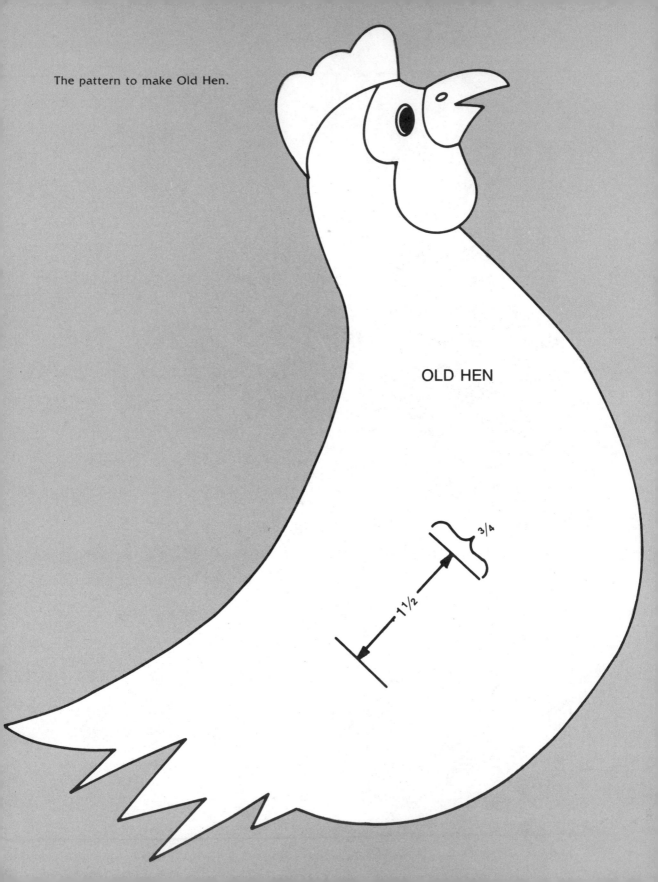

The pattern to make Old Hen.

OLD HEN

3/4

1 1/2

The patterns to make Old Hen's beak, egg, and wing.

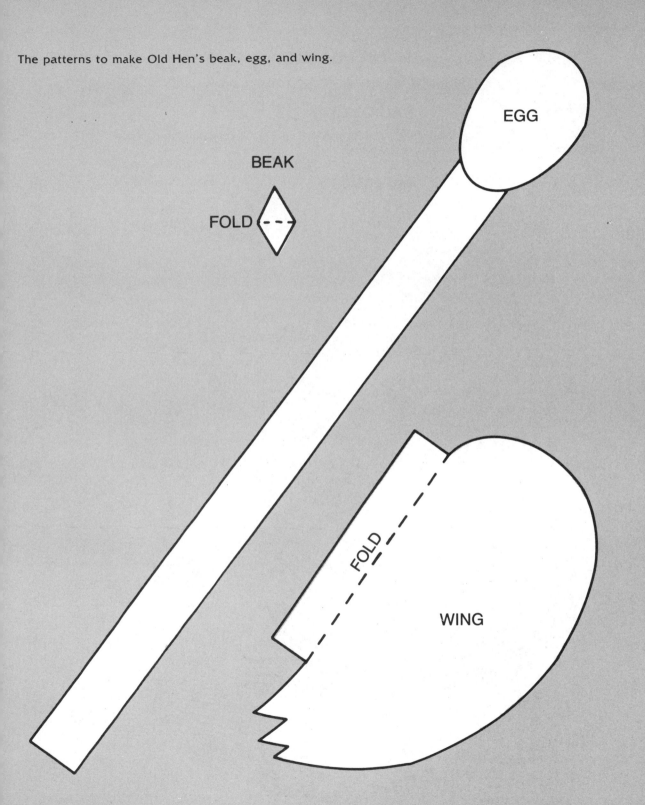

BEAK

FOLD

EGG

FOLD

WING

HALF-PINT BASKET

Use a half-pint whipping cream carton to make this basket.

AGE GROUP

All children will enjoy this craft. With adult help, children as young as 2 will develop patience and coordination skills while making the basket.

MATERIALS LIST

Each child needs:
◇ A half-pint whipping cream carton
◇ Construction paper
◇ A stapler
◇ A pencil
◇ A ruler
◇ Scissors
◇ Glue
◇ A plastic milk lid
◇ Tissue wrapping paper in assorted colors
◇ Easter grass and candy

DIRECTIONS

Wash the cream cartons with warm soapy water. Dry them and cut off the fold-in top, leaving the sides of the carton as tall as possible. The sides should be at least 2 inches tall. Give the children the following instructions:

"Use the pencil and ruler to measure two rectangles on construction paper. One rectangle should be 1½ × 12 inches, and the other should be 2 × 12 inches. Cut them out.

"Wrap the larger rectangle around the sides of the cream carton. Staple in onto the carton. The other rectangle is the handle; stick each end into opposite sides of the carton as far as it will go. Staple the handle on both ends three times to make it secure.

"Cut the tissue wrapping paper into 2-inch squares. Pour a small amount of glue into the plastic milk lid. Press a tissue square around the tip of your finger, forming a paper cup. Dip the bottom of the tissue cup into the glue. Press it onto the basket so that the tissue sticks up like a flower.

"Continue adding tissue squares until the basket and its handle are covered. Let the glue dry. Fill the Half-Pint Basket with Easter grass and candy."

EASTER DOUGH BOYS*

Dutch children traditionally make these charming buns. Your children will love them, too.

AGE GROUP

With an adult's help, any child can make Easter Dough Boys.

MATERIALS LIST

◇ 1¾ cups milk
◇ ¼ cup margarine
◇ 2½ teaspoons sugar
◇ 2 teaspoons salt
◇ 1 package active dry yeast
◇ ¼ cup warm water
◇ 5 to 6 cups flour
◇ 9 small eggs
◇ Raisins
◇ Cotton swabs
◇ Vinegar
◇ Liquid food color

DIRECTIONS

Heat the milk until tiny bubbles form around the edges of the pan. Remove it from the heat and stir in the margarine, sugar, and salt. Cool to lukewarm.

The children can sprinkle the yeast into the warm water in a large bowl. They should stir the mixture until it dissolves. Then they should add the milk mixture and 3 cups of flour, and beat it with a wooden spoon until smooth. Help the children add enough of the remaining flour to make a stiff dough. Then they can knead the dough on a lightly floured surface until it is smooth and elastic. This step takes about 5 minutes.

Put the dough in a greased bowl. Grease the top of the dough and cover it with plastic wrap. Let it rise in a warm place, such as a turned-off oven, until it doubles in bulk, about 1 hour.

Punch the dough down. Divide it into eight equal pieces. To make their Dough Boys, the children can stand around a table that has a plastic cloth on it. Give each child a little pile of flour and a piece of dough. First, the child should roll his dough into a 5-inch oblong. Place a raw, small egg on the dough, a little above the center. Then pretend the egg is the center of a clock. Use scissors to cut slits at 2, 4, 6, 8, and 10 o'clock. The children can gently pull the dough, shaping arms and legs.

Put arms over and across the egg. Shape a round, flat head. Use raisins for eyes, nose, and mouth. Place the finished Dough Boys on greased baking sheets.

Preheat the oven to 400° F. Combine the remaining egg and 1 tablespoon milk in a jar with a tight-fitting lid. Close the lid and shake the jar vigorously. Use this milk-egg mixture to brush on the Dough Boys. Bake 20 minutes, or until a golden brown.

To color the eggs, first remove any oily film from them with a cotton swab and vinegar. Then color each egg with a cotton swab and liquid food color. Do this after the dough has baked.

AFTER-EASTER COOKIES

When the chocolate bunny is no longer wanted, turn it into After-Easter Cookies. Help your child put it in a plastic bag, close it with a twist tie, and hit it with a hammer.

AGE GROUP

This recipe is for anyone who receives chocolate bunnies for Easter and does not want to eat them.

MATERIALS LIST

◇ A large bowl
◇ A wooden spoon
◇ A cookie sheet or two
◇ 1 cup solid shortening
◇ ¾ cup sugar
◇ ¾ cup brown sugar, firmly packed
◇ 1 teaspoon vanilla
◇ 2 eggs
◇ 2¼ cups flour
◇ 1 teaspoon baking powder
◇ 1 teaspoon salt
◇ 1½ cups crispy rice cereal
◇ 1 chocolate Easter Bunny, any size, pounded into small chunks

DIRECTIONS

Show the children how to grease the cookie sheet with their fingers and a little extra solid shortening.

Help them measure the shortening, both sugars, vanilla, and eggs into the large bowl. They can take turns stirring with the wooden spoon until the dough is smooth and mixed well. Help the children measure and add the flour, baking powder, and salt. They should stir these ingredients in with the spoon. Next they should add the cereal and the chocolate pieces and stir until smooth.

Show the children how to drop the dough from a teaspoon onto the greased cookie sheet. Place the cookies about 2 inches apart. Bake in a preheated oven at 350° F for 8 minutes, or until the cookies turn light brown. Remove the hot cookies from the pan. Let them cool on a cooling rack or on a clean kitchen towel spread on the table.

THUMB-PRINT NESTS

Fill each nest with two chocolate-and-candy-coated peanuts for children over the age of 3. Children 3 years and younger can fill their nests with jelly beans or plain candy-coated chocolates.

AGE GROUP

This is an ideal recipe for all ages. Preschoolers learn to measure and stir. Everyone likes to lick their sticky thumbs when they're finished.

MATERIALS LIST

◇ 2 squares unsweetened baking chocolate (2 ounces)
◇ 2 cups flaked coconut
◇ ½ cup sweetened condensed milk
◇ A bowl
◇ A wooden spoon
◇ Cookie sheet covered with wax paper
◇ A small bowl of granulated sugar
◇ Chocolate-and-candy-coated peanuts for children over the age of 3
◇ Jelly beans or plain candy-coated chocolates for children 3 years old and younger (They might choke on the peanuts.)

DIRECTIONS

Put the unwrapped chocolate squares in the top of a double boiler. Melt over boiling water, stirring until smooth. If you have a microwave oven, put the unwrapped chocolate squares in a microwave bowl. Microwave on high for 3 minutes. Stir until smooth.

Help the children measure the flaked coconut, sweetened condensed milk, and melted chocolate into the bowl. They should stir until the mixture is blended.

Help them use a teaspoon to drop pieces of dough the size of a large marble onto the wax paper. They should dip one thumb into a small bowl of sugar, and press the thumb in the center of each piece of dough. This makes a dent that looks like a bird's next. Let them fill their nests with candy.

Refrigerate for 30 minutes, until firm. This recipe makes 36 Thumb-Print Nests.

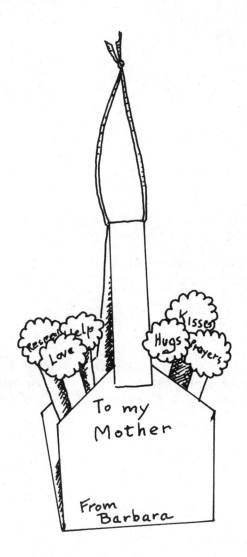

MAY
CRASTS

With May crafts, the children learn to paint with a string and a cotton swab, as well as a brush. They can plant an Egg-Carton Garden inside and later transplant the seedlings outside. A Papier-Mâché Vase can be filled with spring flowers, and cookies shaped like their hands can be given to a preschool or kindergarten teacher as a year-end gift. Maybe they will learn some new skills at the same time.

MOTHER'S DAY BASKET

Give a basket of love to mother on the second Sunday in May.

AGE GROUP

The Mother's Day Basket is designed for children from ages 2 to 7. While making this craft, the children will practice cutting and folding skills. Even the youngest child can learn to glue and to write with an adult's help.

MATERIALS LIST

Each child needs:

◇ A pencil
◇ A ruler
◇ Scissors
◇ Glue
◇ Construction paper in assorted bright colors
◇ A black marker
◇ A 12″ piece of ribbon

DIRECTIONS

Instruct the children as follows: "Use the pencil and ruler to draw the following on colored construction paper: a 9-inch square basket, a handle 1½ x 12 inches, and six flower stems, 1 x 7 inches each. Cut out these pieces.

"Use the pattern to draw six flowers on colored construction paper. Cut out the flowers.

"To make the basket, fold two opposite corners of the square toward the center. Overlap slightly. Fold this in half, forming a five-sided pentagon.

"Glue three flower stems on one side of the basket, and three stems on the other side. Glue one end of the handle to each side of the basket. Use the black marker to write a message such as: *'TO MY MOTHER. FROM, (your name).'* Or you might write, *'HAPPY MOTHER'S DAY. LOVE, (your name).'*

"On each flower, write one of the following gifts for Mom: *HUGS, LOVE, PRAYERS, RESPECT, HELP, KISSES.* If you can think of better gifts to make Mom happy, write your own. Glue a flower on each stem. Tie a 12-inch ribbon in a loop around the handle so the basket can be hung on a doorknob."

FLOWERS
(CUT 6)

The flower pattern for the Mother's Day Basket.

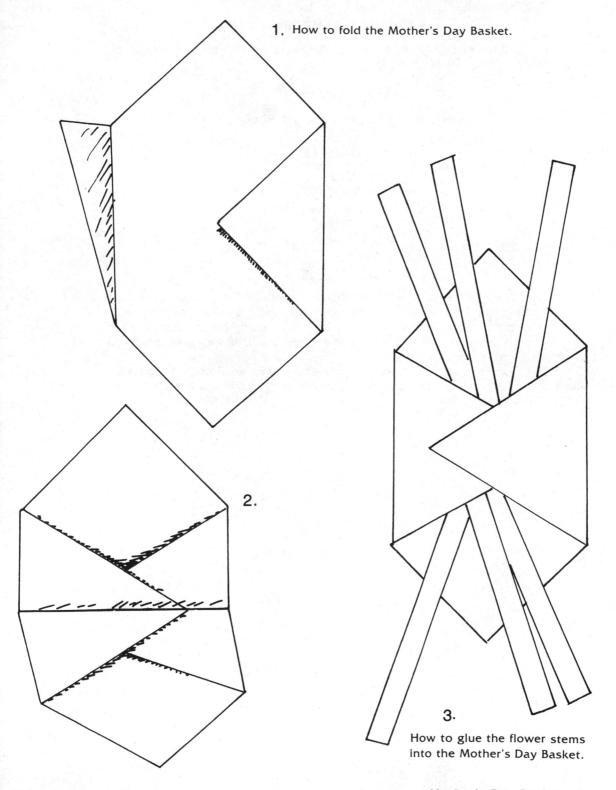

1. How to fold the Mother's Day Basket.

2.

3.

How to glue the flower stems
into the Mother's Day Basket.

STRING PAINTING

Who needs a brush to paint? Try using a string! We save strings from bags of charcoal, cat food, and dog chow. They're perfect for this project.

AGE GROUP

Children of all ages will be interested in the designs created by String Painting.

MATERIALS LIST

Each child needs:
◇ A string 12″ long
◇ White construction paper
◇ Tempera paint
◇ Plastic spoons

DIRECTIONS

Instruct the children as follows: "Fold the construction paper in half like a book. Open it and lay the string inside the paper, with one end of the string sticking out so you can pull it.

"Use the plastic spoons to drop a small amount of paint onto the paper and string. Close the paper with the paint and string inside. Press on it with one hand and gently pull out the string with the other hand.

"Open your string painting and try to imagine what it looks like. Replace the string and add a different color of paint. You can make your string painting with only one color, or you can add several colors. Let it dry open and flat, then hang it up for all to see."

EGG-CARTON GARDEN

The children can plant seeds in empty eggshells, then put them outside when they are big enough.

AGE GROUP

Children ages 2 to 10 will enjoy starting a garden with this activity.

MATERIALS LIST

Each child needs:

◇ A Styrofoam egg carton
◇ 12 eggshells
◇ Scissors
◇ Potting soil or dirt from outside
◇ Flower and vegetable seeds

DIRECTIONS

Tell the children the following: "Cut the lid from the egg carton, using the scissors. Throw the lid away. Fill each egg cup with half of an eggshell.

"Fill each eggshell with potting soil. Plant three seeds in each shell. Water the Egg-Carton Garden and set it in a sunny place. In a few weeks the seeds will sprout. When the seedlings are 2 inches high, cut off the extra ones until only one plant is left in each egg cup.

"When the weather is warm outside, dig a place in your yard for your garden. Transfer the seedlings to your outdoor garden by lifting out plant, eggshell, and all, and planting it in the ground.

"To succeed as a gardener, you must keep your seeds and plants watered at all times. If you forget and let them dry out, they will die."

PAPIER-MÂCHÉ VASE

Turn an empty detergent bottle into a lovely vase for fresh or paper flowers.

AGE GROUP

Children of all ages will be able to make and decorate this vase.

MATERIALS LIST

Each child needs:

◇ An empty detergent bottle
◇ Scissors
◇ 1 cup flour
◇ ¾ cup cold water
◇ A bowl
◇ A spoon
◇ Newspaper cut into strips ½″ x 6″
◇ White paper towels
◇ Tempera paints and brushes
◇ White shoe polish (in a bottle)
◇ Spray shellac (optional)

DIRECTIONS

Papier-Mâché is messy, so have the children cover their work surface with newspapers, and put on a painting coat. Help the children cut off the top portion of the detergent bottle. Mix 1 cup flour and ¾ cup cold water in the bowl. Stir with the spoon until a smooth paste forms.

Tell them to dip strips of newspaper in the paste and smooth them one at a time over the outside of the bottle. Make sure they cover the bottle completely with two layers of strips.

Next, tell them to cut or tear several sheets of white paper towels into strips. Let them dip the strips into the paste and smooth them over the vase to cover up the newsprint.

Tell them to let the vase sit for several days until it is hard and dry. Then have them paint it with liquid shoe polish. Let it dry again.

The children can finish the vase by painting a colorful design on it with tempera paints. Spray it with shellac to make it more durable. The vase can be filled with water to hold fresh flowers, or you can fill it with Egg-Carton Flowers and Tissue Paper Flowers. Directions for making these flowers are found in *Crafts for Kids: A Month-By-Month Idea Book*.

PLASTER CANDY-MOLD MAGNETS

Plaster Candy-Mold Magnets require trips to a hardware store for plaster, a craft store for magnets and paint, and a candy or cooking store for plastic candy molds. This craft is worth the effort, and the molds can be used repeatedly.

AGE GROUP

Anyone who won't put the paint in his mouth can make this craft. Two-year-olds can paint the molded craft. Older children can mix and mold the plaster with a little supervision by an adult. This craft will interest anyone through age 10.

MATERIALS LIST

◇ Newspapers
◇ Aprons
◇ Plastic candy molds
◇ A disposable aluminum casserole pan
◇ A spoon
◇ 2 cups dry plaster of Paris
◇ 1 cup water
◇ Craft magnets ½" in diameter and ¼" thick
◇ Enamel paint
◇ A brush

DIRECTIONS

Tell the children the following: "Spread newspapers on the table, and put on an apron. Mix the plaster and water in the aluminum pan. It will be thin, but will thicken fast, so work quickly.

"Spoon the plaster into the candy molds. As soon as it starts to thicken, sink a magnet into each mold."

The magnet should be sitting above the surface of the mold so that the finished craft can be stuck to the refrigerator. The plaster figures will harden in about 20 minutes. They will easily pop out of the candy molds. Trim each one with a knife. Set them on a newspaper to dry overnight.

The next day, tell the children: "Cover the work area with more newspapers. Put on a painting coat. Paint each plaster figure with shiny enamel paint. Do not paint over the magnet."

Let the Plaster Candy Mold Magnets dry a day or two. Use them to hold notes on the refrigerator.

DIRECTIONS FOR PLASTER HANDPRINTS

Tell the children: "Line a saucer with aluminum foil. Mix the plaster and water. Pour the plaster into the lined saucer. Wait until it starts to thicken.

"When the plaster 'peaks' like meringue when touched, it is ready. Press your hand in hard. Leave your hand in the plaster for a few minutes. Take your hand out, and let the print dry overnight."

WALK-ALONG SPIDER

Choose a warm spring day for this craft, and let the children paint outside. Spread newspapers on their work surface and put an old shirt over their clothes because poster paints stain.

AGE GROUP

While making this delightful spider, children 2 through 6 practice painting, cutting, folding, and gluing. They count to eight while adding the legs.

MATERIALS LIST

Each child needs:

◇ A 9″ white paper plate (Generic plates work well.)
◇ Black poster paint
◇ A brush
◇ Black, white, and red construction paper
◇ Narrow paper ribbon or yarn
◇ Scissors
◇ Glue
◇ A paper punch

DIRECTIONS

Tell the children: "Paint the paper plate all over with black poster paint. Let it dry upside down for at least 2 hours.

"Cut a sheet of black construction paper into eight strips 1¼ × 12 inches each. Fold each strip back and forth to pleat it. With the plate right side up, glue four pleated legs near one edge and four legs near the opposite edge. Use plenty of glue to make the legs stick. Let them dry or they will fall off when you play with your spider.

"Use the pattern to trace two circle eyes onto white construction paper. Add black eyeballs made with a paper punch. Turn the plate over. Glue the eyes on the back of the plate, over-lapping their edges a little. Glue on a red paper oval nose.

"Use any sharp object to punch a hole in the center of the plate. Push a 24-inch piece of ribbon or yarn through the hole. Cut out a piece of construction paper 1 × 3 inches. Squeeze it together in the middle and tie it with the ribbon or yarn under the spider's body. This will prevent the spider from falling off his 'web.'

"Make him walk across the floor by holding onto his web and jiggling him up and down."

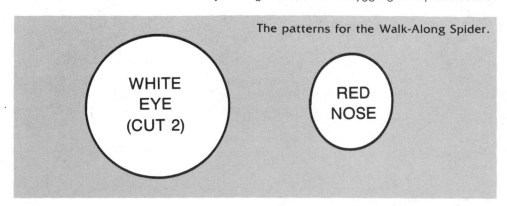

The patterns for the Walk-Along Spider.

WHITE EYE (CUT 2)

RED NOSE

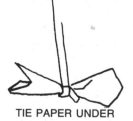

TIE PAPER UNDER

DARYL DOG

Daryl Dog can carry messages, if you stick them in his mouth.

AGE GROUP

This hand puppet is ideal for children from ages 2 to 7 to create. It teaches 2-year-olds the circle shape, plus gluing skills. Children 4 years old and up will practice cutting and following directions.

MATERIALS LIST

Each child needs:
◇ A brown paper lunch bag
◇ Black, white, red, and brown construction paper
◇ Scissors
◇ Glue
◇ A paper punch
◇ A black marker

DIRECTIONS

Use the patterns to trace the following pieces on the construction paper: a black nose, two white eyes, a red tongue, two brown ears, two brown paws, and a brown tail. Cut out these pieces for younger children, but encourage children 4 years old and up to cut their own. Instruct the children as follows:

"Glue the two paws on the front of the bag. Glue the two ears behind Daryl Dog's head. Bend the ears down so he doesn't look like a rabbit.

"Insert the red tongue as far as it will go under the flap of the paper bag. Glue it in place. Curl the tip up a little by rolling it around a pencil.

"Glue the black circle nose and the two white circle eyes on the flap. Overlap the eyes slightly. With the paper punch, make eight black circles from construction paper. Glue three of these on each side of the nose. Use the remaining two circles for eyeballs.

"Fold the tail (as shown on the pattern). Put glue on the folded end. Glue the tail to the back of Daryl Dog.

"Play with your puppet by inserting your hand in the bag and bending your fingers so they fit into the flap. Move your fingers up and down to make Daryl pant, bark, or talk."

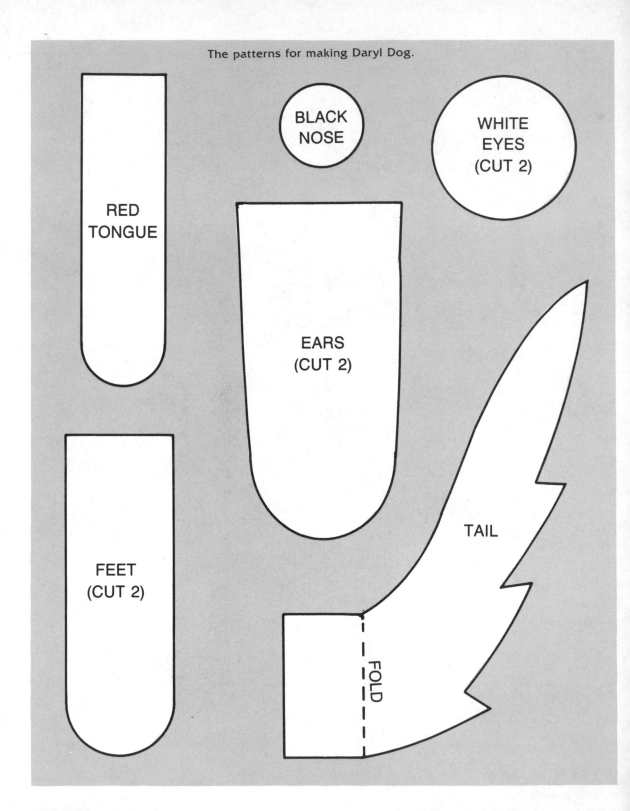

The patterns for making Daryl Dog.

BLACK NOSE

WHITE EYES (CUT 2)

RED TONGUE

EARS (CUT 2)

TAIL

FEET (CUT 2)

FOLD

CANNING-LID COASTERS

This craft recycles the lovely greeting cards people receive. Instead of stuffing them in a drawer or throwing them away, help a child turn them into a gift for someone else.

AGE GROUP

This is a good craft for ages 2 through 10.

MATERIALS LIST

Each child needs:
◇ Wide-mouth canning lids (you can find them in the home canning/freezing section of grocery stores.)
◇ Colorful greeting cards
◇ A pen
◇ Permanent white glue, such as Glue-All
◇ Scissors sharp enough to cut felt
◇ Felt (Buy small pieces in a craft store, larger pieces in a fabric store.)

DIRECTIONS

Give the children the following instructions: "Use the pattern and a pen to draw circles on the greeting cards. Draw one circle for each canning lid. Cut out the circles.

"Trace around the edge of a canning lid onto the felt. Cut out one felt circle for each lid.

"Glue a greeting card circle on the top of each canning lid. Glue a felt circle on the bottom of each lid. Let them dry several hours or overnight."

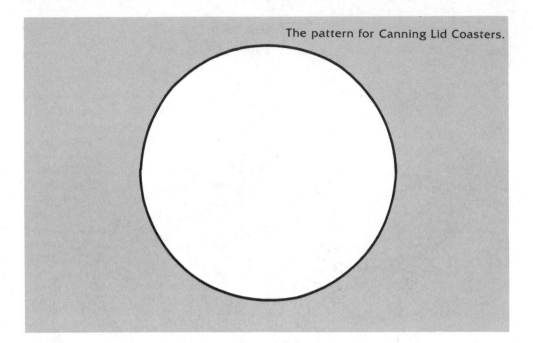

The pattern for Canning Lid Coasters.

DOUGHNUT SHAKE

I included this recipe because it's such a wonderfully easy and delicious dessert that can be made fresh after supper. These doughnuts taste best when hot, but teenage boys will eat them cold, too.

AGE GROUP

An adult must do the cooking because of the hot oil, but children of all ages can shake their doughnuts in the coating of their choice.

MATERIALS LIST

◇ Vegetable oil for deep frying
◇ A large pan or an electric skillet
◇ A candy thermometer
◇ 2 cans of refrigerator biscuits
◇ 3 plastic bags with twist ties
◇ ¼ cup powdered sugar
◇ ¼ cup powdered chocolate drink mix
◇ ¼ cup granulated sugar + 2 tablespoons cinnamon
◇ Slotted spoon
◇ Paper towels

DIRECTIONS

Caution! Keep the children away from the hot oil! Let them wait at the table while you cook at the stove. Tell them that the person who waits best, gets the first doughnut.

Pour vegetable oil into the pan or skillet until it is about 2 inches deep. Heat the oil to 375° F.

Let the children open the cans of biscuits and separate them. They should poke a hole in the middle of each biscuit with their finger. If the biscuit tears in half, tell them to pinch it together again.

When the oil has reached 375°, gently drop in two or three biscuits in a single layer. As soon as they turn golden brown on one side, turn them with the slotted spoon and cook the other side.

Remove the doughnuts from the oil and drain them on paper towels.

Measure powdered sugar into one plastic bag, chocolate drink mix into the second bag, and cinnamon-sugar into the third bag. The children can coat the doughnut by dropping it into the bag of their choice. Close the bag tightly with a twist tie. They can shake the bag, then remove the doughnut and eat it.

Save the left-over coatings to sift on buttered toast for breakfast. Yes, chocolate toast does taste good! Try not to eat too many if you're on a diet.

HANDPRINT COOKIES

These light-brown, mildly spiced cookies are delicious. The dough is sticky, but the baked cookie can be wrapped without breaking easily. Give a right- and left-hand cookie to a teacher with a note saying, "Thank you for helping these little hands learn."

AGE GROUP

Making cookies is fun for all ages. Children will enjoy seeing their handprints bake, and they'll like eating them, too. Handprint Cookies make a good gift for a preschool or kindergarten teacher at the end of the school year.

MATERIALS LIST

◇ A large bowl
◇ A wooden spoon or electric mixer
◇ ½ cup margarine (1 stick), at room temperature
◇ 1 cup sugar
◇ 1 egg
◇ 1 cup molasses
◇ ½ cup water
◇ 7 cups flour
◇ 1 teaspoon baking soda
◇ 1 teaspoon salt
◇ ½ teaspoon ginger
◇ ½ teaspoon nutmeg
◇ ½ teaspoon allspice
◇ ½ teaspoon cloves
◇ A rolling pin with a stockinette cover

DIRECTIONS

Pull up the children's sleeves and let them kneel on chairs. Tie an apron on each child as high up as it will go to cover as much of their clothes as possible.

Help the children measure the margarine, sugar, and egg into the bowl. Use an electric mixer to blend the ingredients thoroughly, or let the children mix them with a wooden spoon.

Blend in the molasses and water. Help the children measure and add the flour, baking soda, salt, ginger, nutmeg, allspice, and cloves. After the children have mixed the dough thoroughly, cover it and refrigerate for at least an hour.

Put a small pile of flour on a breadboard or smooth countertop. Cover a portion of dough with the flour (it will be sticky), and help a child roll it gently until it is ½ inch thick. Spread more flour over the dough surface.

The child can place his hand lightly on the dough while you cut around his hand and fingers with a butter knife dipped in flour. Use a wide spatula to transfer the handprint cookie to a greased baking sheet. Sprinkle the cookie with sugar. Repeat cutting around hands until each child has made two cookies, at least. The children can roll out the remaining dough and cut it into circle cookies with a glass or tuna can dipped in flour.

Bake in a preheated oven at 350° F for 10 to 12 minutes. Loosen the cookies with a spatula and let them cool on the pan or on a cooling rack. They can be frozen.

JUNE
CRABS

June is usually travel month since schools let out for the summer. The first craft for this month is a Car Travel Box, made from cans and boxes, and designed to ease the pains of traveling with small children. Woodsy Bric-A-Brac makes a lovely Father's Day gift, and the Movable Zoo encourages quiet, yet creative, play. On pretty days the children can celebrate summer vacation by having a Muffin-Tin Lollipop party outside.

CAR TRAVEL BOX

A Car Travel Box is perfect for keeping young children busy when they're confined to seat belts and youth seats for long family trips.

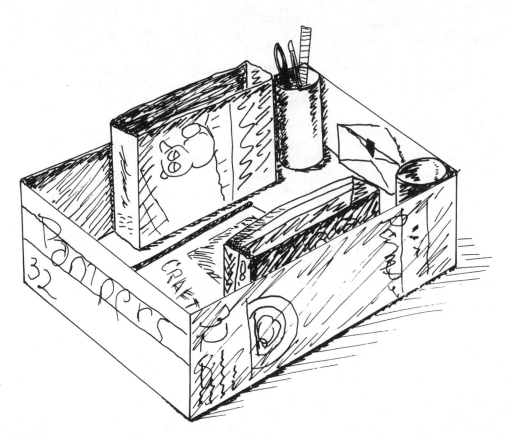

AGE GROUP

This box is useful for preschoolers from ages 3 to 6. It keeps two children separated, gives them lots to do, and keeps their activities neatly organized.

MATERIALS LIST

◇ A large cardboard diaper box (for at least 32 diapers.)
◇ 2 cereal boxes
◇ 2 12-oz. orange juice cans
◇ An envelope 3½″ × 6½″
◇ Wide packaging tape
◇ Scissors
◇ Any or all of the following:
　　A cassette recorder with earphones and recorded books,
　　Drawing paper,
　　Colored pencils,
　　Etch-A-Sketch,
　　Magic Slates,
　　Sticker books,
　　Magic Pen Painting Books (that can be colored with a water pen.),
　　View Master and slides, Story books

DIRECTIONS

The Car Travel Box must be put together by an adult. Then the children can help choose items to fill it.

Begin by cutting the front out of the diaper box. Cut a long side from each cereal box. Tape a cereal box inside the diaper box, with the cut sides up. The cereal boxes can be filled with drawing paper, sticker books, Magic Slates, and story books, as well as Magic Pen Painting Books.

Tape an orange juice can on each side of the diaper box, with the open end up. The cans will hold colored pencils, water pens for the Magic Pen Painting Books, and drawing sticks for the Magic Slates.

Tape the envelope inside the diaper box at one end. It will hold View Master Slides.

In the middle of the diaper box, arrange a cassette recorder with earphones, Etch-A-Sketch, View Master, and cassette tapes.

The items chosen for the Car Travel Box generally will not ruin the inside of the car. If your children can be trusted with crayons, include some of them, too. Remember, though, that crayons melt in a hot, parked car.

To use this box, put it between two children who are safely fastened in infant or youth seats or in seat belts. When you reach your destination, put the box away with everything in it. The children should be allowed to play with the things in the box only while they are in the car so the activities will remain special to them.

WOODSY BRIC-A-BRAC

If children can find a few trees and gather pine cones and acorns, then add a seed or two and some walnut shells, they can make an attractive item to set on the coffee table or desk.

AGE GROUP

Children from ages 2 to 10 will enjoy making this craft.

MATERIALS LIST

Each child needs:
◇ Newspapers
◇ A circular piece of wood, any size, or a cross section of a tree, cut 1½" thick
◇ Dried things such as pine cones, acorns, sea shells, walnut shells, and seeds
◇ A 4-oz. squirt bottle of white glue
◇ Scissors
◇ A marker
◇ Felt (Found in fabric and hobby stores.)

DIRECTIONS

Tell the children to spread newspaper on their work surface. Let them squirt glue on one side of the wood circle and press the pine cones, shells, seeds, and nuts into the glue. Tell them to dribble the glue over the top of everything. This step might use up the entire 4-ounce bottle. Glue will drip down the sides of the wood circle, but this is to be expected. Let the glue dry for several days until it looks shiny and translucent like varnish. Then have the children use a marker to trace around the wood onto the felt.

Tell them to cut out the felt circle and glue it to the bottom of the wood. When the glue on the felt has dried completely, Woodsy Bric-a-Brac is ready to display.

TEDDY TURTLE

His head pulls in when he is shy; pokes out again when food is nigh.

AGE GROUP

This is a good craft for children 2 years old and up.

MATERIALS LIST

For each child you need:
◇ A pencil
◇ Scissors
◇ Glue
◇ Dark green and light green construction paper
◇ A hole punch
◇ A black marker
You also need a razor blade.

DIRECTIONS

Instruct the children as follows: "Use the pencil and the patterns to trace the following onto dark green construction paper: four feet, a head, and a tail. Cut out the pieces. Use the pattern to trace the turtle's shell onto light green construction paper. Cut out the shell."

FOR ADULTS ONLY: Use the razor blade to make a 1¼-inch slit in the shell, as shown on the pattern. Then tell the children:

"Decorate the shell with a black marker. Draw lines on the feet and on the tail. Make a white eye with the hole punch, and draw a black eyeball on it. Glue the eye to Teddy's head. Add a mouth and a nostril with the marker.

"Glue two feet at the bottom of the shell so they hang down. Glue the other two feet under the shell and a little behind the first feet so you can see them. Add the tail.

"Insert the head in the slit. The long neck should be hidden behind the turtle's shell. Push his head in and out by holding onto the hidden end of the neck."

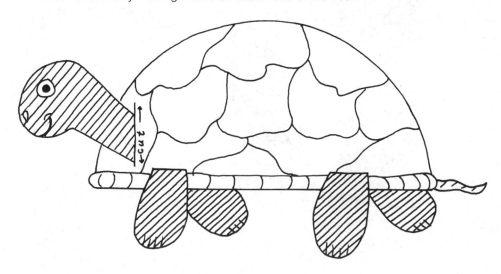

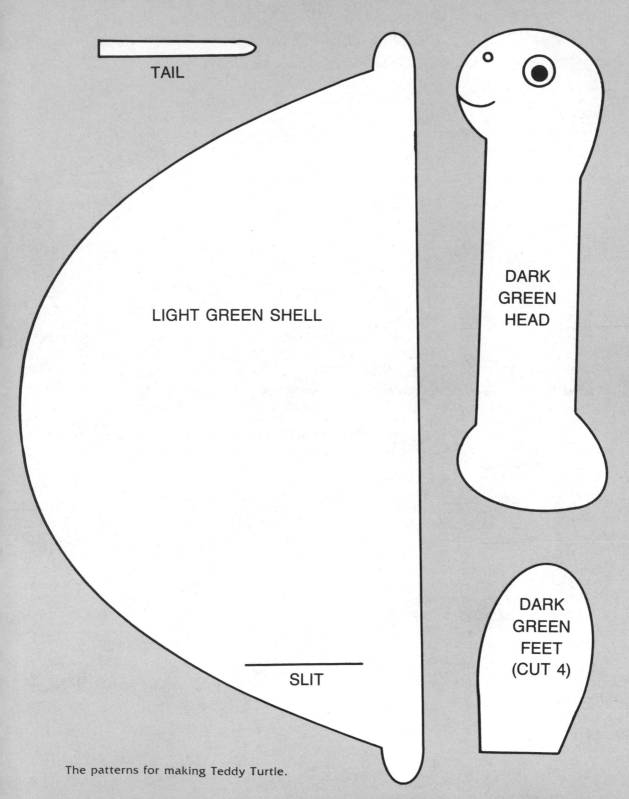

TAIL

LIGHT GREEN SHELL

DARK GREEN HEAD

SLIT

DARK GREEN FEET (CUT 4)

The patterns for making Teddy Turtle.

GINNY GIRAFFE

She has a long neck and long legs, too. To see her in person, go to the zoo.

AGE GROUP

Children 2 years old and up will learn about a giraffe's long legs and neck, spots, horns, and tasseled tail. They will practice cutting, gluing, coloring, braiding, and following directions as they put Ginny together.

MATERIALS LIST

For each child you need:
◇ A pencil
◇ Scissors
◇ Glue
◇ Yellow construction paper
◇ A paper punch
◇ 3 pieces of yarn, 6″ each
◇ A black marker
◇ Brown and red crayons
You also need a razor blade.

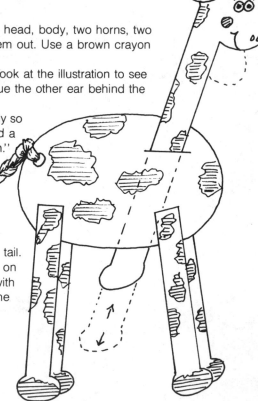

DIRECTIONS

Tell the children: "Use the pencil and patterns to trace the head, body, two horns, two ears, and four legs onto yellow construction paper. Cut them out. Use a brown crayon to color spots on all the pieces.

"Draw a face on Ginny Giraffe with a black marker. Look at the illustration to see how to do it. Glue one ear on the left side of the head. Glue the other ear behind the right side of the head.

"To assemble Ginny Giraffe, glue two legs on the body so they point downward. Glue two legs under the body and a little in front of or behind the first legs so you can see them."

FOR ADULTS ONLY: Use the razor blade to make a 1-inch slit in the body, as shown on the pattern.

Then tell the children: "Insert the neck through the slit. Hide the rounded end behind her body. Make her head move up and down by moving the hidden end.

"Use the paper punch to make a hole for the giraffe's tail. Put the three pieces of yarn through the hole, tying them on with a knot. Braid them. Tie the braid near the bottom with an extra piece of yarn. Separate the threads of yarn at the end of the braid to make a fluffy tassel."

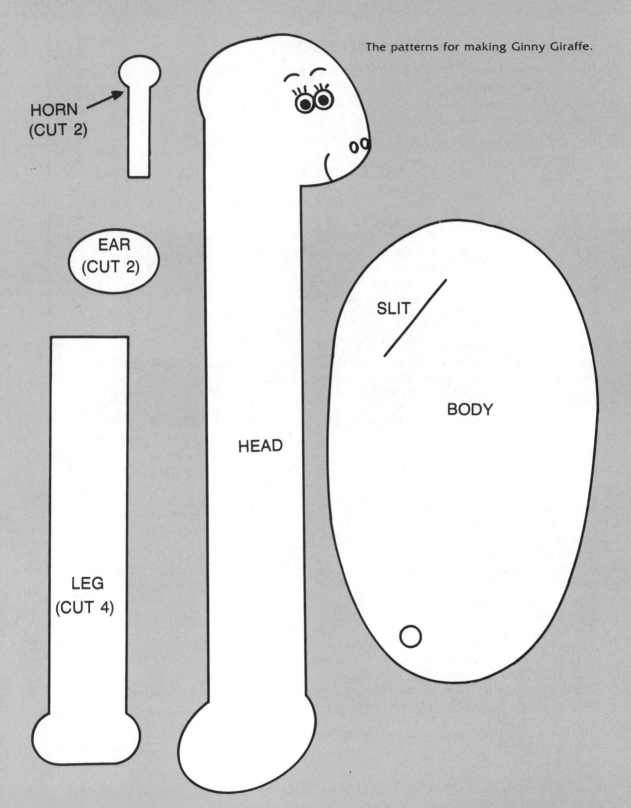

The patterns for making Ginny Giraffe.

HORN
(CUT 2)

EAR
(CUT 2)

SLIT

BODY

HEAD

LEG
(CUT 4)

ERNIE ELEPHANT

Another circle body, four more rectangle legs, and a trunk that reaches and moves make Ernie a popular elephant.

AGE GROUP

Ernie Elephant is a nice craft for children 2 years old and up.

MATERIALS LIST

For each child you need:
◇ A pencil
◇ Scissors
◇ Glue
◇ Gray and white construction paper
◇ A hole punch
◇ Yarn, cut into a 4″ piece
◇ Black and red markers
You also need a razor blade.

DIRECTIONS

Instruct the children as follows: "Use the pencil and the patterns to trace the following onto gray construction paper: two ears, four rectangle legs, a trunk, and a circle body. Cut out the pieces. Use the pattern to trace two tusks and two eyes onto white construction paper. Cut them out.

"To assemble Ernie Elephant, glue two legs at the bottom of the body so they hang over the edge of the circle. Glue the other two feet under the body and a little ahead of the first feet so you can see them.

"Glue two circle eyes on the upper left of the body. Put them close together. Glue one ear to the right of the eyes. Glue the other ear to the left of the eyes and under the body, partly sticking out."

FOR ADULTS ONLY: Use the razor blade to make a ¾-inch slit in the body, as shown on the pattern. Then tell the children:

"Glue one tusk on the left side of the slit. Glue the other tusk beneath the slit. Fold the fat end of the trunk (as shown on the pattern) and insert it in the slit. Unfold it. The fat end should be hidden behind the elephant's body.

"Make a hole in the body (as shown on the pattern) with a hole punch. Tie on the yarn for a tail. Tie a knot 1 inch from the end of the tail. Separate the individual strands of yarn at the end to make a tassle.

"Use the black marker to draw eyeballs, eyebrows, and feet. Use the red marker to draw a mouth beneath the tusks."

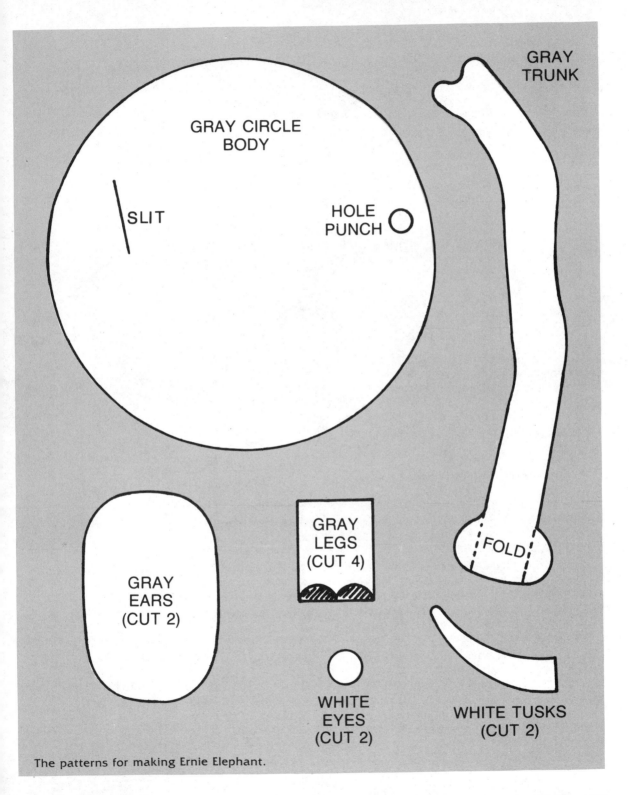

The patterns for making Ernie Elephant.

HELEN HIPPOPOTAMUS

Her body is a circle, her legs are four rectangles, and her ears wiggle to chase away flies.

AGE GROUP

This is a good craft for children 2 years old and up.

MATERIALS LIST

For each child you need:
◇ A pencil
◇ Scissors
◇ Glue
◇ Gray and white construction paper
◇ Red and black markers (The skinny water-based markers work best.)
◇ A paper punch
◇ A 4″ piece of yarn
You also need a razor blade.

DIRECTIONS

Tell the children: "Use the patterns to trace a circle body, four rectangle legs, and a head onto gray construction paper. Cut these pieces out.

"Fold a piece of gray paper in half. Place the ear pattern on the fold. Cut this out through both thicknesses of paper. Unfold the ears. They will be attached in a V shape.

"Use the patterns to trace two circle eyes onto white paper. Cut them out.

"To assemble Helen Hippopotamus, first glue two rectangle legs on top of the circle body, and sticking downward (as shown in the illustration).

"Second, glue two rectangle legs under the circle body and slightly behind the front legs so you can see them.

"Third, glue the head onto the body. It can cover the tops of the front legs a little."

FOR ADULTS ONLY: Use the razor blade to cut through the body, outlining the top of the head as shown on the pattern. The child can insert the ears in this slot so the V is hidden behind the body, and the ears stick up above the head. Wiggle the ears by moving the V back and forth and up and down. Then tell the children:

"Before adding the eyes, use the black marker to draw a line across the middle of each one. Draw half an eyeball below this line. This gives Helen a sleepy look. Glue the two eyes on the head.

"Add eyelashes, eyebrows, and nose holes with the black marker. Draw a mouth under the head with a red marker. Use the red marker to color the cheeks and the insides of the ears.

"Use the hole punch to make a hole in the body (as shown on the pattern). Insert the piece of yarn through this hole and tie it in a knot. Tie another knot 1 inch from the end of the yarn. Pull the end of the yarn apart into separate threads to make a tassled tail. Trim with the scissors."

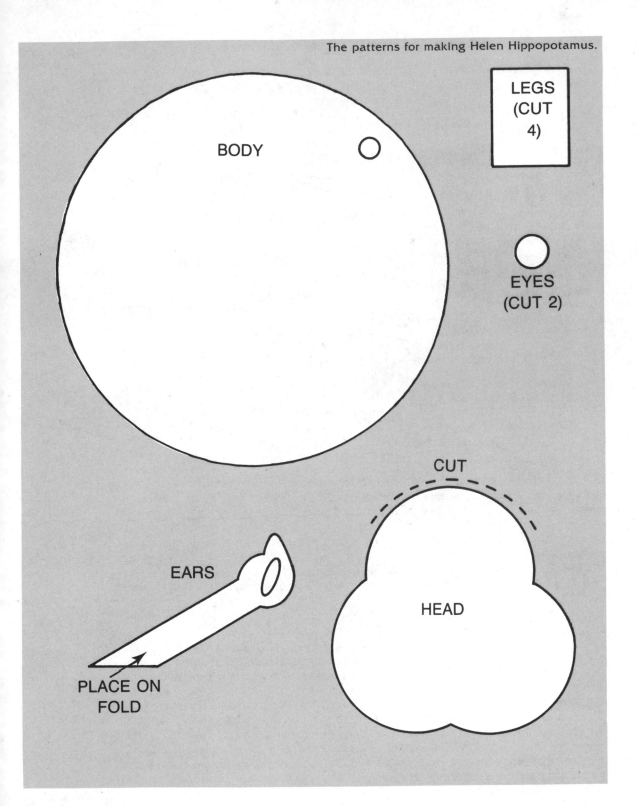

The patterns for making Helen Hippopotamus.

LEGS (CUT 4)

BODY

EYES (CUT 2)

CUT

EARS

HEAD

PLACE ON FOLD

LARRY LION

His mouth opens so he can eat; his tail is braided nice and neat.

AGE GROUP

This is a good craft for children 2 years old and up.

MATERIALS LIST

For each child you need:
◇ A pencil
◇ Scissors
◇ Glue
◇ A paper punch
◇ A black marker
◇ Yellow, brown, black, and white construction paper
◇ 3 pieces of yarn, 6" each
You also need a razor blade.

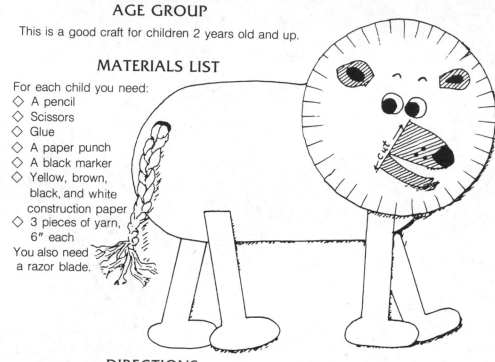

DIRECTIONS

Instruct the children as follows: "Use the pencil and patterns to trace a head, body, and four legs onto yellow construction paper. Trace two ears, a snout, and a mouth onto brown construction paper. Trace two white eyes and a black nose. Cut out everything.

"Fringe the head by making shallow cuts all around it with scissors. This is the mane. Bend the fringes with your fingers so the mane curls a little. Glue the head on one end of the body."

FOR ADULTS ONLY: Use the razor blade to make a ½-inch slit in the head, as shown on the pattern. Since the head is glued to the body, make the slit go through the body also. Then tell the children:

"Glue two feet on the body so they stick downward. Glue the other two feet under the body and a little behind or in front of the first feet so you can see them.

"Glue the brown snout above the slit and to the right of it. Glue two white circle eyes close together and above the snout. Add two black eyeballs made with the paper punch. Glue the black nose to the snout. Glue on two brown ears. With a black marker, draw three dots on the snout, eyebrows, and a center on each ear.

"Use the paper punch to make a hole for the lion's tail. Tie three pieces of yarn together at one end. Braid them and tie the braid at the end with an extra piece of yarn. Separate the individual threads of yarn to make a fluffy tassle on the end. Insert the tail through the hole in the body so that the tassle hangs down and the knot is hidden behind the body.

"Insert the lion's mouth through the slit. Hide the rounded end behind his body. Make his mouth open and shut by moving the hidden end up and down."

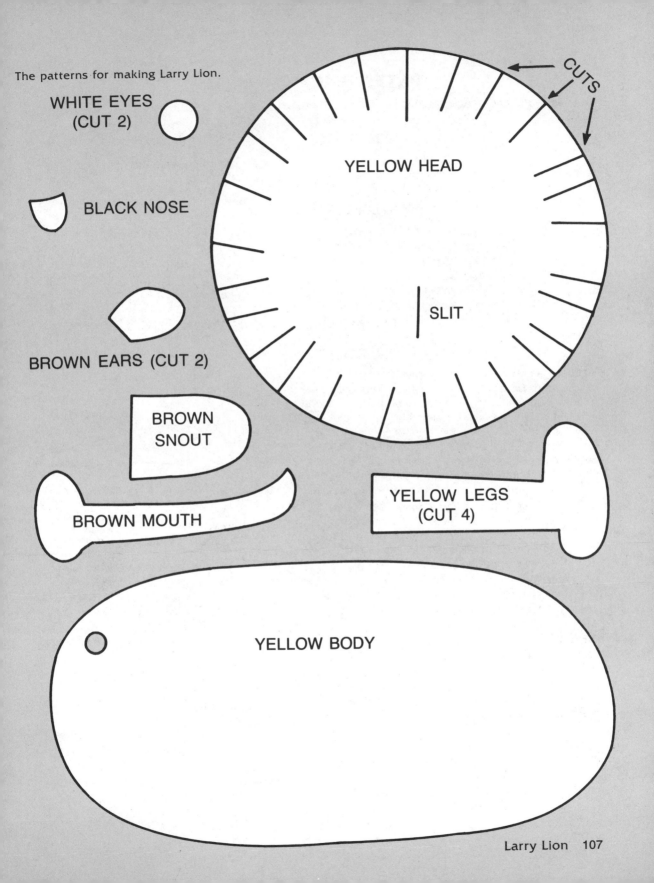

The patterns for making Larry Lion.

WHITE EYES
(CUT 2)

BLACK NOSE

BROWN EARS (CUT 2)

BROWN
SNOUT

BROWN MOUTH

YELLOW HEAD

CUTS

SLIT

YELLOW LEGS
(CUT 4)

YELLOW BODY

PATTY PELICAN

She has two bright orange legs. Lift her wing to find her eggs.

AGE GROUP

Children 2 years old and up will learn what a pelican is. They will practice cutting, gluing, following directions, and putting things together as they make Patty Pelican.

MATERIALS LIST

For each child you need:
◇ A pencil
◇ Scissors
◇ Glue
◇ Brown, orange, and white construction paper
◇ A black marker

You also need a razor blade.

DIRECTIONS

Instruct the children as follows: ''Use the pencil and patterns to trace a body, a tail, and a wing onto brown construction paper. Use the patterns to trace two feet, an upper beak, and a lower beak onto orange construction paper. Trace three eggs and two eyes onto white paper. Cut out all the pieces.

''Glue the two legs under the bottom of the body. Let the fat feet stick down so Patty can walk. The orange upper beak and lower beak fit together. Glue them on the right side of Patty Pelican's head. Glue the eyes near the top of the head. They should be touching or lapping over the upper beak. Glue the tail under the left side of the body so that it sticks out.''

FOR ADULTS ONLY: Use the razor blade to make a 1-inch slit in the body, as shown on the pattern. Then tell the children:

''Insert the wing tab in the slit. Fold the tab and glue it down behind the pelican. Lift the wing and glue three eggs under it.

''Use a black marker to draw eyeballs, wing feathers, tail feathers, toes, and a nose hole. If you want your pelican to be a boy bird, pretend he is keeping the eggs warm while the mother is out shopping.''

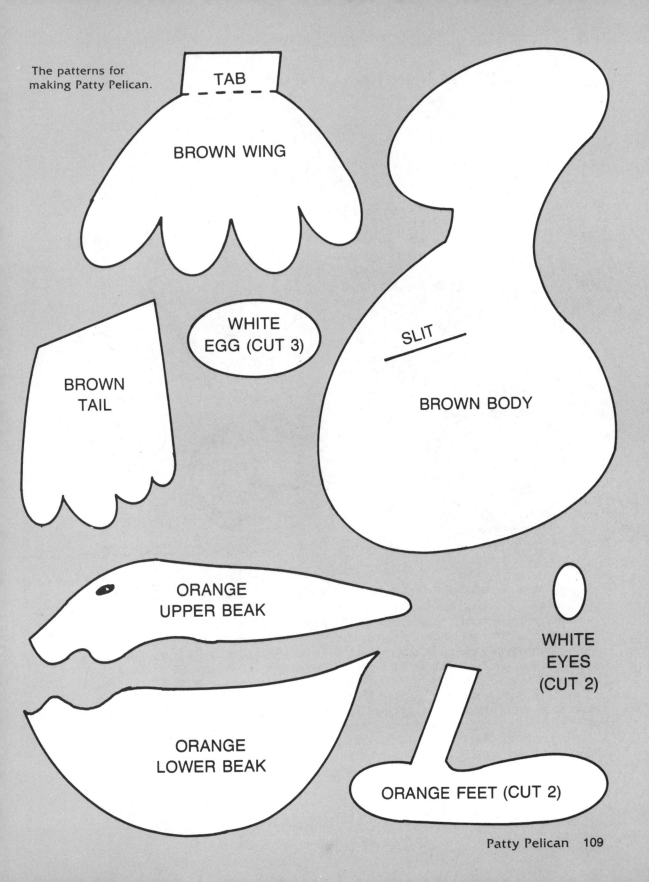

The patterns for making Patty Pelican.

TAB

BROWN WING

WHITE EGG (CUT 3)

BROWN TAIL

SLIT

BROWN BODY

ORANGE UPPER BEAK

WHITE EYES (CUT 2)

ORANGE LOWER BEAK

ORANGE FEET (CUT 2)

MUFFIN-TIN LOLLIPOPS

These all-day suckers have a strange shape, but taste great!

AGE GROUP

Adults must do the cooking because of the hot syrup, but all children will love eating these lollipops. Let the children help measure the ingredients into the pan. They can also add a few gumdrops or candy corn to the greased muffin tin before the lollipop syrup is poured in.

MATERIALS LIST

◇ Nonstick cooking spray
◇ A 6-cup teflon-coated muffin tin
◇ A 2-quart cooking pot
◇ A wooden spoon
◇ 1 ½ cups sugar
◇ 6 tablespoons corn syrup
◇ 1 ½ tablespoons vinegar
◇ 3 tablespoons water
◇ 2 tablespoons butter
◇ 6 popsicle sticks

DIRECTIONS

Spray the muffin tin with nonstick cooking spray. Help the children measure the sugar, corn syrup, vinegar, and water into the pan.

Cook on high heat, stirring constantly, until the mixture begins to boil. Reduce the heat to medium. Let the candy simmer, stirring occasionally, until it reaches the hard-ball stage. Test for this stage of doneness by dropping a small amount of the candy into a bowl of cold water. Feel the candy with your fingers. When it forms a hard ball, it is ready (290° F on a candy thermometer).

Remove the saucepan from the heat. Stir in the butter. Pour the hot syrup into the six muffin cups. Press a popsicle stick into each. Let the lollipops cool and harden. The sticks will try to float to the top; press them in as the candy cools and thickens.

To remove the lollipops from the muffin tins, slide a table knife between the candy and the inside of each muffin cup. This will force the lollipop to pop out.

Store each lollipop in a plastic sandwich bag until someone wants to eat it.

BANANA PUDDING

Banana Pudding is the first thing my children learn to cook, after toast, that is.

AGE GROUP

Any child who can stir can make pudding. This is a perfect recipe for ages 2 through 10.

MATERIALS LIST

◇ A large bowl
◇ A wooden spoon
◇ Butter knife
◇ Instant pudding, 4-serving size
◇ 2 cups cold milk
◇ Banana
◇ Vanilla wafers

DIRECTIONS

Tie an apron on your child and wash his hands. Let him open the pudding and pour it into the bowl. Help him add the milk. He can stir until the mixture becomes smooth and thick.

Help him peel a banana. Let him cut the banana into pieces with the butter knife. He can stir the banana pieces into the pudding. Then he can make a pretty design on top the pudding with vanilla wafers.

Cover the pudding with plastic wrap and refrigerate. At dessert time, let the "chef" help serve Banana Pudding to the family. This recipe serves four.

JULY CRAFTS

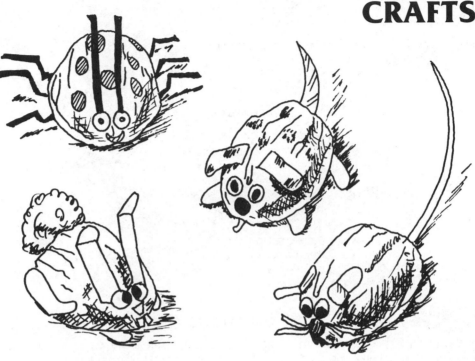

July crafts begin with Nutty Pets, made of walnut shells and construction paper. As a volunteer Art Mom at our local school, I helped 27 eight-year-olds make their own pets, and they sent me the following notes:

> Dear Mrs. Dondiego,
>   Thank you for coming in and helping us do ar project. They really are cute. I gave my bunny one to my friend because she was sick and she gave me a sucker in return.
>   Love, Christina

> Dear Mrs. Dondiego,
>   My mom thought my jerbil was real. I made a cage for my jerbil. I made a house for the rest of them.
>   Love, Laura

> Dear Mrs. Dondiego,
>   Thank you for helping us make the Nutty Pets they were fun! I told my mom I brought home a pet and she said rightaway to let it go! But I told her I made it and she was releaved.
>   Love, Jeanette

NUTTY PETS

Buy walnuts at the grocery store to make these cuties. Open each walnut by inserting a table knife in the large end of the nut and pulling the knife along the seam to force it into halves.

AGE GROUP

This craft is designed for children 5 and up. The small pieces are difficult for younger children to work with.

MATERIALS LIST

Each child needs:
◇ Walnut shells, opened into perfect halves
   (Large walnuts split into halves more
   easily than small ones.)
◇ Construction paper in assorted colors
◇ Scissors
◇ Glue
◇ A paper punch
◇ Cotton balls
◇ A black marker
◇ A black crayon

DIRECTIONS

The children can use the patterns provided, or they can create their own version of a Nutty Pet. Give the children the following instructions, depending on which pet they want to make.

"To make the ladybug, cut six skinny legs 1 inch long each. On a scrap of paper, squirt a drop of glue to dip the legs into. Dip one end of each leg in the glue, and put three legs under one side of the shell, partly sticking out, and three legs under the other side. Use the hole punch to make eleven circles from red construction paper. Dip each circle in the glue and put it on the back of the bug. Glue two white hole-punch eyes on the front of the bug. Draw on eyeballs with a black marker. Glue on two skinny antennae, ¾ inch long each, sticking up above the eyes.

"To make the rabbit, use the pattern to trace and cut out two front legs, two back legs, and two ears. Glue the two front legs under one end of the shell, partly sticking out. Glue a back leg on each side of the shell near the back. Add two white hole-punch eyes. Draw on eyeballs with a black marker. Glue on two ears, a tiny paper snip for a nose, and two tiny white square teeth. Glue on a little piece of cotton for a tail.

"To make the gerbil, use the pattern to trace and cut out two front feet, two back feet, two ears, and a tail. Glue the two front feet under the shell near the front and partly sticking out. Glue the two back feet under the shell near the back and partly sticking out. Glue the tail under the back of the shell. Curl it upward slightly. Make two white eyes with the hole punch. Draw on eyeballs with a black marker. Glue them on the front of the gerbil. Add a black hole-punch nose. Glue four skinny paper whiskers, ½ inch long, so they stick out from the nose, two on each side. Fold each ear in half. Dip half the ear in glue, put it on the gerbil's head, above his eyes. Repeat with the other ear. Bend them so they stand up.

"To make the dog, use the pattern to trace and cut out four paws, two ears, and a tail. Glue the two front feet under the shell near the front and partly sticking out. Glue the two back feet under the shell near the back and partly sticking out. Fold the tail (as shown on the pattern) and dip the folded end in glue. Stick it on the back of the dog. Glue the ears to the top of the dog's head, near the front. Add white hole-punch eyes and a black hole-punch nose. Glue a tiny strip of red construction paper under the front of the shell so that it makes a little tongue sticking out. Use the black marker to draw eyeballs. Use a black crayon to draw spots on the ears and on the dog's back.

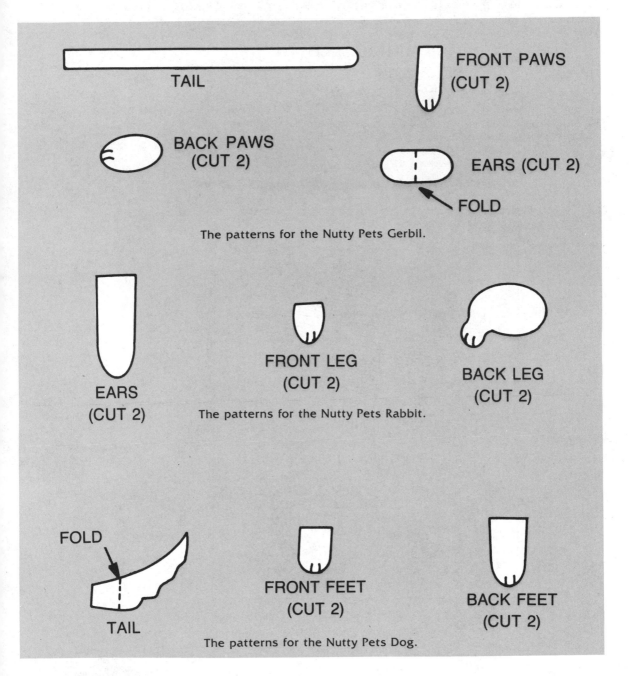

TAIL

FRONT PAWS
(CUT 2)

BACK PAWS
(CUT 2)

EARS (CUT 2)

FOLD

The patterns for the Nutty Pets Gerbil.

EARS
(CUT 2)

FRONT LEG
(CUT 2)

BACK LEG
(CUT 2)

The patterns for the Nutty Pets Rabbit.

FOLD

TAIL

FRONT FEET
(CUT 2)

BACK FEET
(CUT 2)

The patterns for the Nutty Pets Dog.

SUMMER SHOWERS PICTURE

Cut out pictures of flowers from seed catalogs and magazines.

AGE GROUP

This craft is designed for children ages 2 to 6. It gives them practice in cutting with scissors. It also teaches them the triangle shape, the letter **J**, and the color red. They also get lots of practice in eye-hand coordination as they glue on "raindrops."

MATERIALS LIST

Each child needs:
◇ A pencil
◇ Red, blue, and white construction paper
◇ Scissors
◇ Glue
◇ A paper punch
◇ A seed catalog or magazine with pretty flower pictures

DIRECTIONS

Instruct the children as follows: "Use the pattern to trace five triangles and a **J** umbrella handle onto red construction paper. Cut out the pieces.

"Lay the five triangles on a sheet of white construction paper, near the top of the page. Put the triangle points together and spread out their bases, keeping them overlapped slightly to make them look like an umbrella. Glue them in place.

"Glue on the umbrella handle. Make sure it is turned the right way to look like the letter **J**.

"Cut out pretty flowers from catalogs. Glue them at the bottom of the page, under the umbrella. Use the paper punch to make lots of blue paper raindrops. Glue them all over the picture."

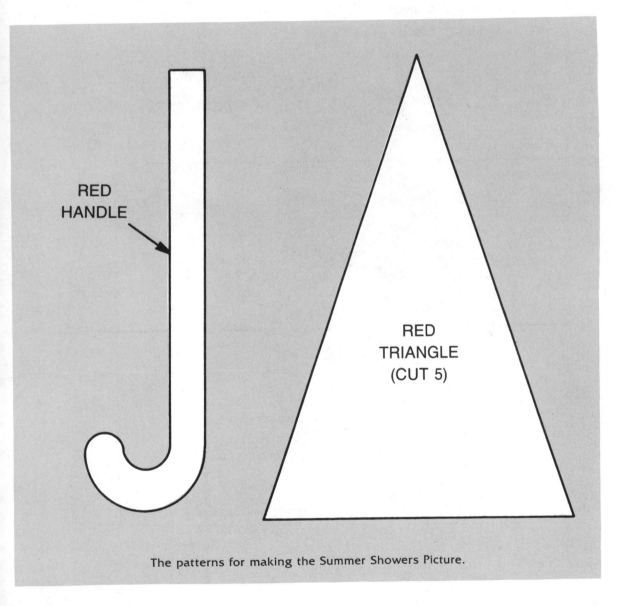

RED
HANDLE

RED
TRIANGLE
(CUT 5)

The patterns for making the Summer Showers Picture.

CIRCLE PIG

He won't be found in any barnyard, but the Circle Pig looks great taped to the wall or the refrigerator.

AGE GROUP

Youngsters 2 years old and up can be taught the circle shape while making this pig. Cut out the circles for children under the age of 4, and let them assemble it.

MATERIALS LIST

Each child needs:
◇ A pencil
◇ A ruler
◇ Blue, white, red, and pink construction paper
◇ Scissors
◇ Glue
◇ A toilet-paper roll
◇ A black marker
◇ 1 pipe cleaner

Fig. C-1. (Left) The finished Paper Wind Socks.

Fig. C-2. (Below) Paper Wind Socks in flight.

Fig. C-3. The Egg Carton Toy Bin.

Fig. C-4. Sweet Gum Spiders.

Fig. C-5. The Leprechaun Hats.

Fig. C-6. Making the Styrofoam Cup Bell.

Fig. C-7. Making a Doily Ball.

Fig. C-8. Making the Pine Cone Bird Feeder.

Fig. C-9. Making the Shapes Candle.

Fig. C-10. Making cookies.

Fig. C-11. Party scene.

Fig. C-12. Making the Turkey Jar.

Fig. C-13. Nutty Pets.

Fig. C-14. The Salt Box Pig.

Fig. C-15. NickNack Chicks.

Fig. C-16. Patty Pelican.

Fig. C-17. Hanging the Paper Lantern.

Fig. C-18. Making the Cereal Necklace.

Fig. C-19. Be-a-Bunny.

Fig. C-20. Making the Salt-Box Rocket.

DIRECTIONS

Give the children the following directions: "Use the patterns to trace a large circle on pink construction paper, a medium-sized circle on white paper, and a small circle on pink paper; or trace around a cereal bowl, a large jar lid, and a coffee cup to make three circles of different sizes. Cut out the circles.

"Trace around the end of the toilet-paper roll onto red construction paper to make the smallest circle for the pig's snout. Cut out the piece. Cut the toilet-paper roll into a 1-inch cylinder.

"Use the pattern to trace two feet onto pink construction paper, and two ears onto red paper. Cut them out.

"Glue the largest pink circle in the middle of a sheet of blue construction paper. Glue the medium-sized white circle on top of the large pink one. Glue the small pink circle on top of the white one and near its bottom edge.

"Glue the two pink feet under the largest circle so they stick out at the bottom. Put glue on the straight end of each red ear. Insert the two ears under the top of the small pink circle so they stick straight up like rabbit ears. Next fold the ears down over the pig's face.

"Wind the pipe cleaner around a pencil to make a curly tail. Straighten out one end and put glue on it. Stick the glued end behind the largest circle so that the tail sticks straight up.

"Apply glue around one edge of the toilet-paper roll. Place the roll, glued edge down, on the small pink circle, near its bottom. Apply glue to the top edge of the roll. Lay the smallest red circle on this glued edge.

"Let the pig lay flat and dry completely. Then use a black marker to draw eyes above the snout. Draw two circles on the snout so the pig can breathe. Color the tips of the hooves."

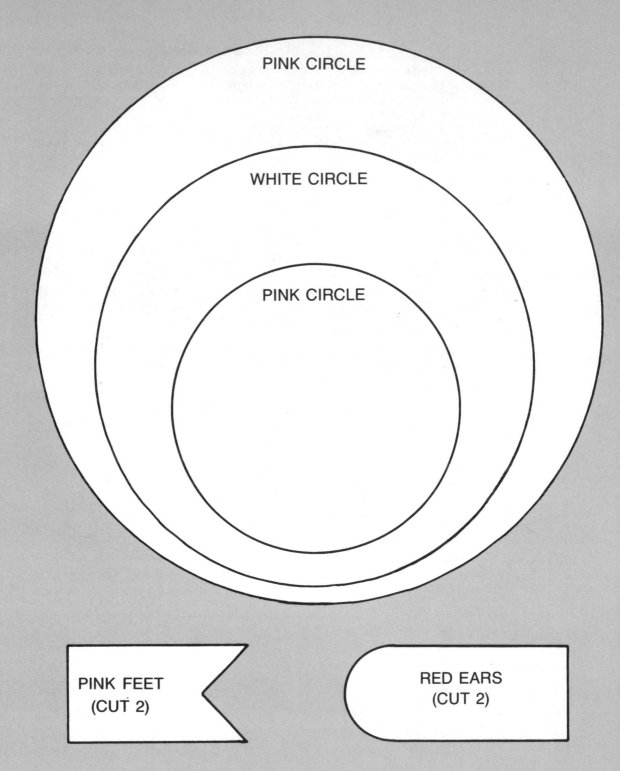

The patterns for the Circle Pig.

LOOK WHAT'S IN A CIRCLE!

Start with a circle made of paper, cut out a slice, and create nine creatures plus a tulip. The Circle Creatures also can be made from paper plates and saucers.

AGE GROUP

This craft is simple enough for a 2-year-old and creative enough for a 10-year-old and all the ages in between.

MATERIALS LIST

Each child needs:
◇ A pencil
◇ Construction paper
◇ Scissors
◇ Glue
◇ A black marker
◇ A cotton ball

DIRECTIONS

Instruct the children as follows: "Use the pattern and a pencil to draw ten circles onto construction paper. Cut them out. Cut a **V** from each circle (as shown on the pattern).

"Look at the illustrations to create a pig by cutting the **V** into two pieces, gluing them on as ears, and adding a circle snout and a skinny paper tail. Make the tail curl by wrapping it around a pencil or your finger.

"To create a dog, cut the **V** into two equal pieces and glue them on as ears. Use the pattern to draw and cut out a paper tail, and draw the face with a black marker.

"Fish #1 is made by gluing the **V** under the circle. The eye is made of a small circle of black paper. Fish #2 is made by gluing the *V* on top of the circle, and adding a white circle eye with a black eyeball. Fish #3 is made by turning the circle in the opposite direction and adding the **V** as a fin. Fringe the fin, glue on a white circle eye, and draw a tiny black mouth.

"To create a cat, cut the **V** into two equal pieces and glue them behind the circle with only the tips sticking out for ears. Use the pattern to draw and cut out a paper tail. Add white circle eyes. Draw the face with a black marker.

"Make the rabbit by cutting the **V** into two equal pieces. Trim the narrow point of each piece to make a rounded paw. Glue the paws under the rabbit so they stick out a little. Use the pattern to draw two ears on paper. Cut them out. Add the ears and a cotton-ball tail with glue.

"To make the owl, cut the **V** into two equal pieces. Glue them behind the circle with only the narrow tips showing for ears. Add white paper circle eyes and a drawn-on face.

"Create the tulip by gluing the **V** under the circle so the narrow tip sticks up. Add a green paper stem and two green leaves."

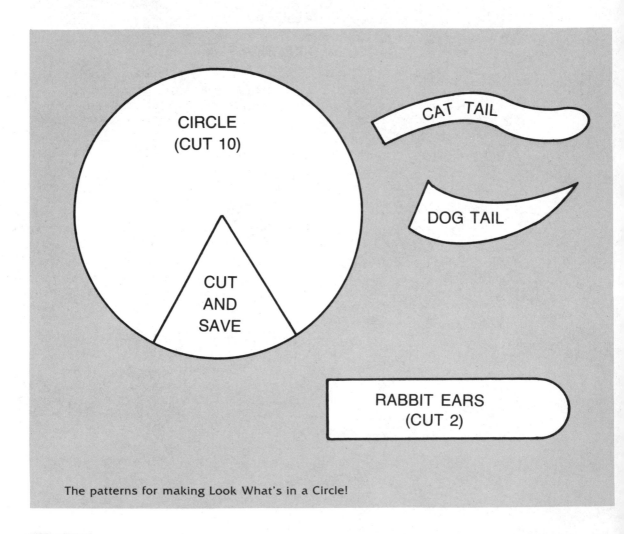

The patterns for making Look What's in a Circle!

MAKING FINGER PAINT

Containers for cottage cheese and sour cream make perfect jars for mixing and storing homemade finger paint.

AGE GROUP

Bring out the painting coats, cover the table with newspaper, and let everyone from ages 2 to 10 make paint designs with their fingers.

MATERIALS LIST

◇ 1 cup liquid laundry starch
◇ 1 cup Ivory Snow laundry soap
◇ Tempera paint
◇ Mixing bowl
◇ Rubber spatula
◇ 4 plastic containers with lids
◇ 4 plastic spoons or popsicle sticks
◇ Newspaper
◇ White paper
◇ Wet sponge

DIRECTIONS

Help the children measure the liquid starch and the soap powder into a mixing bowl. They can stir this mixture with a rubber spatula until smooth.

Divide the mixture into four plastic containers. Add about one tablespoon tempera paint to each container. One container can hold red paint, one can be tinted blue, and so on to make four different colors of finger paint. Let the children stir the finger paints with plastic spoons until they are well mixed.

Put painting coats on the children, and spread newspapers on their work surface. Give each child a piece of white paper. Wet the paper a little by rubbing over it with a wet sponge. Put a tablespoonful of finger paint on each child's paper. They can spread the paint around in any way they wish. Add a spoonful of paint of a different color. Let them spread that around. When the children are ready to let their paintings dry, they can make a design, draw a picture, or write their name in the paint with their fingers.

This paint dries slowly, so let the finished papers lie flat overnight before hanging them up.

HOOTY-HOOT OWL PUPPET

Hooty-Hoot is very cute. He has big eyes and wings to boot.

AGE GROUP

Children from ages 2 to 4 will learn cutting and gluing skills as they put this craft together. Older children can trace and cut the puppet pieces themselves. Hooty-Hoot teaches all children how to make a hand puppet from a piece of paper.

MATERIALS LIST

Each child needs:
◇ A pencil
◇ A ruler
◇ Scissors
◇ Glue
◇ A 9″ × 12″ piece of brown construction paper
◇ Yellow, orange, brown, black, and white construction paper
◇ A paper punch

DIRECTIONS

Instruct the children as follows: "Fold the sheet of brown construction paper toward the center, 3 inches on each side. Turn the folded paper over. Use the pattern to draw the top of the owl's head. Cut the top to round it (as shown by the pattern).

"Use the patterns to draw two circle eyes on black construction paper. Draw two brown wings and two orange feet. Cut out the pieces.

"Fold a piece of yellow paper in half. Place the mask pattern on the fold. Draw around the pattern. Cut out through both thicknesses of paper. Unfold the mask.

"Cut the beak the same way. Fold orange paper in half, place the beak pattern on the fold, cut out, and unfold the beak.

"To assemble Hooty-Hoot, glue on the yellow mask. Add black circle eyes. Glue a white circle, made with the paper punch, in the top corner of each eye. This will look like a highlight instead of an eyeball.

"Glue on the beak between the eyes. Since an owl has a hooked beak, curl the top of it around your finger.

"Glue a wing on each side of the body. Glue the feet to the bottom of the puppet. Turn the puppet over. Overlap the back paper and glue to close. Also glue around the top of the head.

"To work the puppet, slip your hand through the bottom. You can make other animals or people with this method by using different colors of paper, and adding eyes, ears, arms, whiskers, or whatever you can think of."

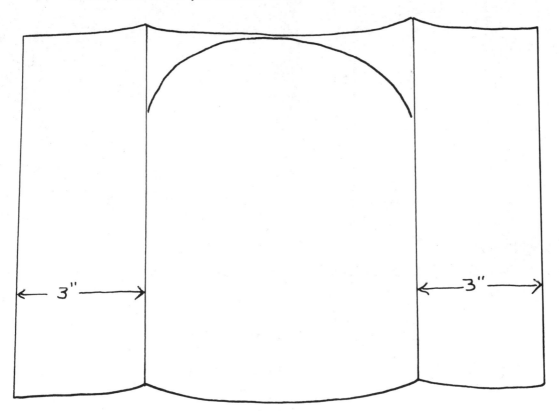

How to fold the paper to make Hooty-Hoot Owl Puppet.

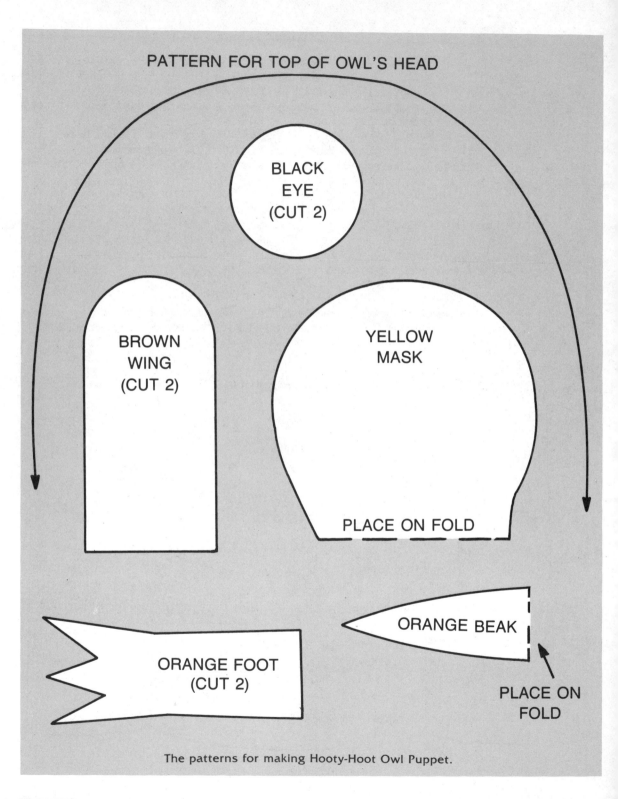

The patterns for making Hooty-Hoot Owl Puppet.

CHOCOLATE NOODLES

Chocolate Noodles are unbelievably delicious and easy to make.

AGE GROUP

Everyone can make these goodies, from the youngest to the oldest.

MATERIALS NEEDED

◇ A large bowl
◇ A wooden spoon
◇ A cookie sheet covered with wax paper
◇ A teaspoon
◇ 2 cups (12 ounces) chocolate chips
◇ 3 ½ cups (6 ounces) chow mein noodles

DIRECTIONS

Pour the chocolate chips into the top of a double boiler. Melt over hot water, stirring until smooth. If you have a microwave oven, pour the chocolate chips into a large microwave-proof bowl. Microwave on high for 3 minutes. Remove from the oven. Let the children stir the chips with a wooden spoon until smooth.

Help the children measure and add 3½ cups chow mein noodles to the melted chocolate. They can take turns stirring until all the noodles are covered with chocolate.

The children can use a teaspoon to drop the noodles in small mounds onto the cookie sheet covered with wax paper.

Refrigerate 30 minutes until the chocolate hardens, then eat. Store in a tightly closed container in the refrigerator or freezer.

CROUTON STICKS

These spicy bread sticks are a delicious snack. If Mom wants to try the recipe, they're great with salads, too.

AGE GROUP

This craft is great with children of all ages, including large groups.

MATERIALS LIST

◇ 1 cup lukewarm water
◇ 1 package dry yeast
◇ ¼ cup sugar
◇ ¼ cup shortening
◇ ¾ teaspoon salt
◇ 4 cups flour
◇ 1 stick (¼ lb.) margarine, divided
◇ A large bowl and a wooden spoon
◇ A large jelly-roll pan

SPICE MIX

½ cup parmesan cheese
1 teaspoon paprika
1 teaspoon seasoned salt
1 teaspoon Italian seasoning

DIRECTIONS

Preheat the oven to 450°F. Measure ⅓ cup (5⅓ tablespoons) margarine onto the jelly-roll pan, and let it melt in the oven while the oven is heating. Remove the pan from the oven as soon as the margarine is melted.

The children can measure 1 cup lukewarm water into the large bowl. Add the dry yeast and stir to dissolve.

Next they should add the sugar, shortening, salt, and flour. They should stir this with a wooden spoon until it is mixed into a smooth dough. If you prefer, you can combine these ingredients in a mixer bowl and knead for 2 minutes with a dough hook. Then give the dough to the children. Add flour if it is sticky.

This recipe makes enough dough for four children to make eight crouton sticks each. Given each child one-fourth of the dough and a little pile of flour to keep the dough from sticking to the tabletop.

Tell the children to divide their dough into eight equal pieces. Tell them to roll each piece into a snake 10 inches long. Lay the snakes side by side in the jelly-roll pan that is coated with melted margarine. The sticks may touch each other.

There is enough room in the jelly roll pan for 32 crouton sticks, crowded together. When the pan is full, melt the remaining margarine (3⅔ tablespoons) and brush it over the sticks.

Combine the ingredients for the spice mix in a glass jar. Close the lid and shake to mix.

Sprinkle all the Spice Mix evenly over the crouton sticks. Bake at 450°F for 20 minutes. Remove from the oven, and use a metal spatula to separate the sticks.

Put each child's crouton sticks in a paper lunch bag to eat or to share.

CROUTON STICKS FOR 30

With this recipe, 30 children can make alphabet letters, pretzel shapes, stick men, or what-ever. The taste is delicious.

AGE GROUP

This craft is for groups of children of all ages.

MATERIALS LIST

◇ A large pot or roasting pan
◇ Several baking sheets
◇ A pan for melting butter
◇ A pastry brush
◇ 4 cups lukewarm water
◇ 3 packages dry yeast
◇ 1 cup sugar
◇ 1 cup shortening
◇ 1 tablespoon salt
◇ 16 cups flour
◇ 1 pound butter or margarine
(Do not add to dough)

SPICE MIX:

2 cups parmesan cheese
4 teaspoons paprika
4 teaspoons seasoned salt
4 teaspoons Italian seasoning

DIRECTIONS

The day before the baking project, measure the lukewarm water into the large pot or roasting pan. Add the yeast, stirring to dissolve. Add the sugar, shortening, salt, and flour. Stir this as best you can to form a smooth dough.

Cover with plastic wrap and refrigerate overnight. Combine the ingredients for the Spice Mix in a glass jar. Close the lid and shake to mix.

The next day, give each child a piece of wax paper or baking paper to work on. Put a little pile of flour on the child's paper to keep his dough from sticking while he works with it. Punch down the dough and divide it among the children.

Tell the children to divide their dough into four equal pieces. Tell them to roll each piece into a snake about 10 inches long. They can leave the snake straight, tie it in a pretzel shape, or whatever.

Grease several large baking sheets, or line them with baking papers.

Preheat the oven to 450° F. Melt the margarine or butter over low heat in a pan.

The children can lay their crouton sticks on the baking pans. If baking papers are used, write the child's initials on the paper next to his dough.

Use a pastry brush to coat the crouton sticks with melted butter. Sprinkle all the Spice Mix over them.

Bake at 450° F for 20 minutes. Give each child his crouton sticks in a paper lunch bag.

AUGUST
CRAFTS

School starts in August, and it's also a good month to make crafts outside. Gather the children around the picnic table in the backyard, or give each a TV tray on the back porch. Then try Spray Painting and Marble Painting, which are neater than you might think. Keep the flour out of the kitchen by making Clay Dough and Alligator Bread outside, too. Finish the month by taking the children apple picking, if that's possible where you live, and making homemade applesauce.

SPRAY PAINTING

Spray painting gives the effect of spatter painting without the mess.

AGE GROUP

All ages will enjoy creating art with this fun and easy method.

MATERIALS LIST

Each child needs:
◇ An empty detergent box 8″ × 11″ × 2½″
   (Sometimes called "Giant Size")
◇ 1 tablespoon tempera paint (A .75 oz. jar)

◇ ¼ cup water
◇ An empty nonaerosol spray bottle
◇ White construction paper
◇ Straight pins
◇ Anything that will leave a design, such as
   leaves, paper shapes, or other small objects

DIRECTIONS

Instruct the children as follows: "Cut the top of the detergent box on three sides so it flaps open or shut. You will slide the paper in and out through this opening.

"Cut one side out of the detergent box. Measure the paint and the water into the spray bottle. Put the lid on the bottle and shake to mix.

"Slide a sheet of white paper into the box. Arrange the items that you have chosen for your design on the paper. If possible, anchor them to the paper with straight pins.

"Spray the paper lightly. Too much paint will drip and run. Leave the painting in the box until it is dry. Then remove the pins and other objects, slide the painting from the box, and hang it up to admire."

MARBLE PAINTING

Marbles rolling in a box create a crazy-art picture.

AGE GROUP

All ages should try this method of painting at least once.

MATERIALS LIST

Each child needs:
◇ An empty detergent box 8″ × 11″ × 2½″
◇ White construction paper
◇ Cellophane tape
◇ Tempera paints in different colors
◇ Plastic spoons
◇ Several marbles

DIRECTIONS

Give the children the following instructions: "Cut the top of the detergent box on three sides so it flaps open and shut. You will slide the paper in and out through this opening.

"Cut one side out of the detergent box. Slide a sheet of white paper into the box. Anchor the paper with cellophane tape. Tape the flap of the box closed.

"Use the plastic spoons to drop a small amount of tempera paint onto the paper. Put several marbles in the box. Tip the box back and forth, up and down, so the marbles will roll through the paint, spreading the paint in designs on the paper.

"Add some different colors of paint. Roll the marbles again. Let the painting (and marbles) dry in the box. Then slide the painting from the box and make up a name for it.

"Wash the marbles in hot, soapy water and save them for another day.

MAKING CLAY DOUGH
AND PRETEND FOODS

Baked shapes of clay dough dry hard and white. They can be painted with tempera paint or water colors. Coat with clear nail polish or spray shellac for a shiny finish. One word of caution: Do not lay the finished foods on furniture or carpeting. The paints could stain them.

AGE GROUP

Children as young as 2 years old will enjoy squeezing and patting the dough into "cookie" shapes. Older children can make a whole gourmet meal that will delight any doll.

MATERIALS LIST

◇ 1 cup salt
◇ ½ cup + 2 tablespoons water
◇ ½ cup cornstarch
◇ A saucepan or microwave bowl
◇ A wooden spoon
◇ Wax paper
◇ Aluminum foil
◇ A baking sheet
◇ A garlic press
◇ A round toothpick
◇ Tempera paint or water colors and brush
◇ Clear nail polish or shellac (optional)

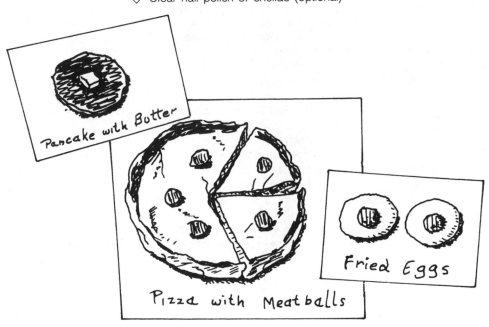

Pancake with Butter

Pizza with Meatballs

Fried Eggs

DIRECTIONS

Mix salt, water, and cornstarch in a saucepan. Cook over high heat, stirring constantly, until the mixture thickens and becomes stiff. Remove from heat. Stir with a wooden spoon until smooth.

If you have a microwave, mix the salt, water, and cornstarch in a microwave bowl. Cover with wax paper. Microwave on high for 2 minutes. The mixture will be very thick. Stir it with a wooden spoon until smooth.

After the clay dough has cooled, the children can make the following "foods" on wax paper. Cover a baking sheet with aluminum foil. Transfer the foods to the sheet, and bake at 350° F for 30 minutes. Let the figures dry in the turned-off oven for several hours.

Instruct the children as follows, depending on what foods they want to make:

"Hot dog and bun: Press a ball of clay into a 1-inch circle. Curl it up to form the bun. Roll out a fat 1-inch hot dog. Place it in the bun. Bake, then paint the hot dog brown.

"Fried Egg: Press a ball of clay into a 1-inch circle. Top it with a ¼-inch ball, flattened slightly. After baking, paint the ball yellow.

"Frying Pan: Press a ball of clay into a 2-inch circle. Add a coil of clay around the top edge of the circle, forming a rim. Add a 1-inch handle shaped like a hot dog.

"Serving Dish: Press a ball of clay into a 2-inch circle. Add a coil of clay around the top edge of the circle to form a rim. Add two balls opposite each other to make handles.

"Sausage: Roll out ½-inch hot dog shapes. Paint brown after baking.

"Bacon: Make a small roll of clay. Flatten it with your fingers. Paint it with brown and yellow stripes after baking.

"Pizza: Press a ball of clay into a 2-inch circle. Bake, then paint it red. Let the paint dry. Add brown dots for pepperoni.

"Spaghetti: Force clay through a garlic press onto aluminum foil. Add several small balls for meatballs. Bake. Paint a little bit of red on the spaghetti to look like sauce. Paint the meatballs brown.

"Glass of Milk: Roll a fat coil 1 inch long. Flatten the top and bottom so it will stand up. Bake.

"Plates: Press balls of clay into 2-inch circles. Bake. Paint any color.

"Fork: Roll out a 1-inch coil. Flatten one end with your fingers. Dent the flat end with a toothpick in two places to form fork tines. Then bake.

"Knife: Roll out a 1-inch coil. Slightly flatten half of the coil to form a knife blade. Bake.

"Spoon: Roll out a 1-inch coil. Squeeze one end into a circle. Bake.

"Pork Chop: Roll a 1-inch ball. Slightly flatten to make a thick pork chop. Pull out one end to shape a curved bone. Paint brown after baking.

"Chicken Drumstick: Roll a 1-inch ball. Pull and squeeze the clay out to make the chicken bone. Dent the bone on the end. Bake and paint brown.

"Mashed Potatoes and Gravy: Roll a 1-inch ball. Flatten the bottom. Dent the middle with your finger. Bake. Paint the dented middle with brown paint to look like gravy.

"Peas: Roll 12 or more tiny (⅛-inch) balls. Stick them together in a mound. Bake and paint green.

"A Vase with Flowers: Roll a fat coil 2 inches long. Flatten the bottom so it will stand up. Poke a round toothpick in it several times to hollow it out. Bake and paint. Make flowers by gluing construction paper shapes to the ends of toothpicks. Break the toothpicks so they are the desired length, and stick them in the finished vase.

"Use a powder box for a doll's dinner table. Cover the top of the box with a lace handkerchief or a tissue 'tablecloth.' Set the table with the plates, knives, forks, spoons, and vase of flowers. Cut out a rectangle of plain paper 1 x 3 inches. Fold it in half to make a tiny menu. On this menu, write the names of the foods you have made. Invite your dolls out to dinner."

CUTOUT COW

She may not give milk, but she does stand up by herself.

AGE GROUP

With adult help, children 2 years old and up can make Cutout Cow.

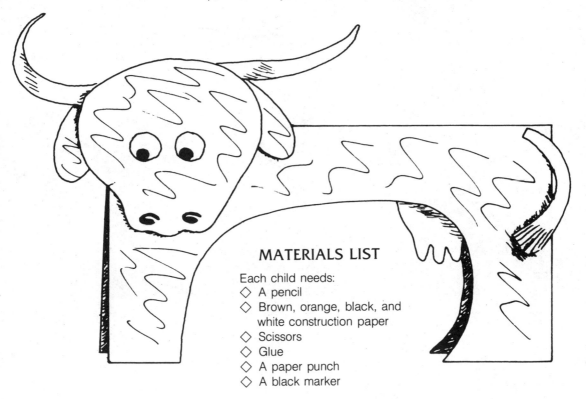

MATERIALS LIST

Each child needs:
◇ A pencil
◇ Brown, orange, black, and white construction paper
◇ Scissors
◇ Glue
◇ A paper punch
◇ A black marker

DIRECTIONS

Instruct the children as follows: "Fold a sheet of brown construction paper in half to make a rectangle 6 x 9 inches. Use the pattern to draw the cutout shape on the open edge of this rectangle. Cut the shape out to form the cow's body and legs. The pattern also tells you where to glue on the head and tail when you are ready.

"Use the second pattern to trace the cow's head, two horns, two ears, and tail on brown construction paper. Cut these pieces out. Fringe the end of the tail so the cow will have a tassle.

"Use the pattern to trace an udder on orange paper and two circle eyes on white paper. Cut them out. Use a hole punch to make two black circle eyeballs.

"Glue the tail on the cow's body (as shown on the pattern). Open the folded body and glue the udder between the back legs so that it can be seen a little bit.

"Glue the horns on the back of the cow's head so they are pointing outward. Glue an ear on each side of the head below the horns so that the rounded edge is pointing downward.

"Add the white eyes and black eyeballs. Use the black marker to draw nostrils at the end of the cow's head. Her mouth does not show, so try not to draw one.

"Spread her legs apart to make her stand up."

The pattern to make the body of the cutout Cow.

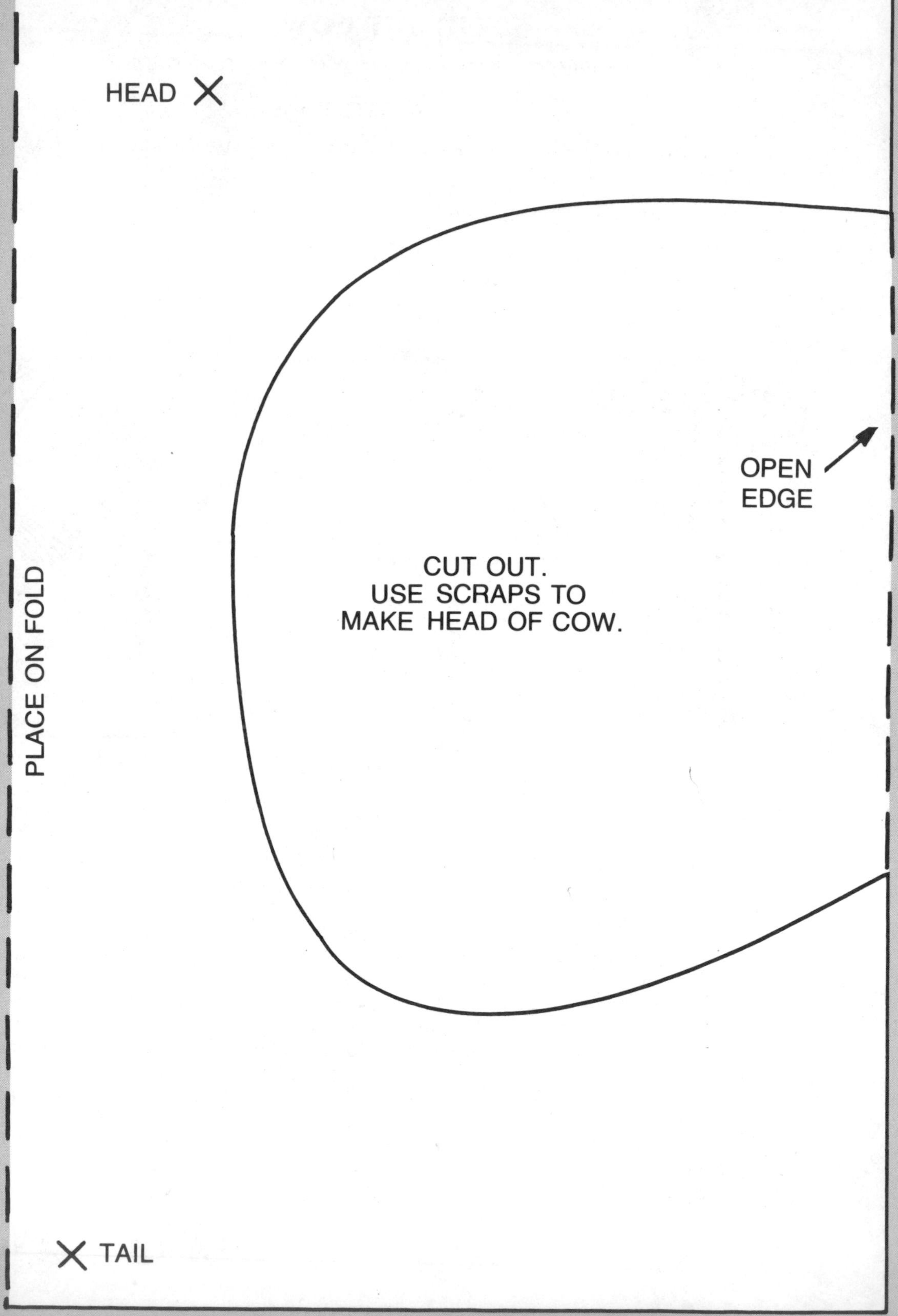

HEAD ✕

OPEN
EDGE

PLACE ON FOLD

CUT OUT.
USE SCRAPS TO
MAKE HEAD OF COW.

✕ TAIL

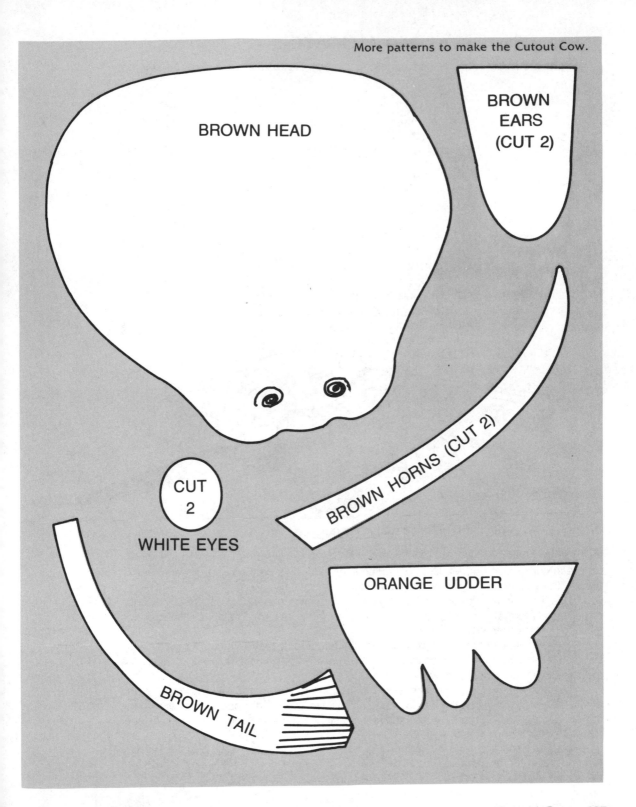

BROWN HEAD

BROWN EARS (CUT 2)

BROWN HORNS (CUT 2)

CUT 2

WHITE EYES

ORANGE UDDER

BROWN TAIL

ALFRED ALLIGATOR

Alfred is a durable critter made of a toilet-paper roll. His tail moves back and forth.

AGE GROUP

This is a good craft for preschoolers, ages 2 to 5.

MATERIALS LIST

Each child needs:
◇ A toilet-paper roll
◇ A pencil
◇ A ruler
◇ Scissors
◇ Glue
◇ A paper punch
◇ A black marker
◇ A paper fastener (Look in the stationery
   section of grocery stores and drugstores.)
◇ Green construction paper
◇ A small stapler
   (optional)

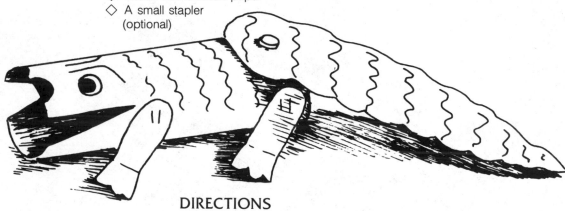

DIRECTIONS

Instruct the children as follows: "Use the pencil and ruler to draw a rectangle 4½ × 6 inches on green construction paper. Cut out the rectangle. Put glue on the rectangle and wrap it around the toilet-paper roll to cover the roll completely.

"Use the pattern to trace a tail onto green construction paper. Cut out the tail. Use the paper punch to make a hole in the tail (as shown on the pattern). Draw wavy lines on the tail with a black marker. Set it aside.

"Cut a **V** shape on both sides of one end of the paper roll to make a mouth for the alligator. Use a black marker to draw fierce eyes. Add eyebrows and nostrils. Draw wavy lines across the back of Alfred to look like alligator skin.

"Use the paper punch to make a hole in the top of the alligator, ⅛ inch from the end of the roll. Place the tail on the back with the holes lined up. Insert a paper fastener through the tail and the roll. Spread out the tabs of the fastener inside the roll. The paper fastener allows the tail to move back and forth.

"Use the pattern to trace four legs onto green construction paper. Glue or staple the legs to the sides of the alligator so he can slither around. A small stapler will fit inside the paper roll so the legs can be stapled on. Staple each leg twice for durability."

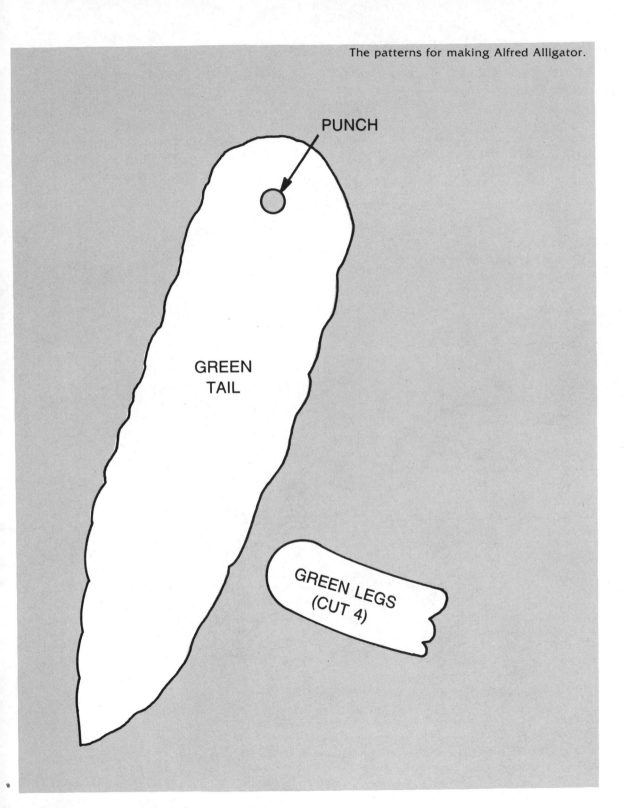

PUNCH

GREEN
TAIL

GREEN LEGS
(CUT 4)

PAPER-PLATE CRAB

This realistic crab has eight jointed legs, two big claws, and eyes on a stalk. He can be fed through his open mouth.

AGE GROUP

Children 2 through 10 can make this craft. Preschoolers can learn to count to 8. They practice coloring, cutting, and gluing. Older children like to create their own crabby creatures.

MATERIALS LIST

Each child needs:

◇ A 9″ white paper plate (Generic plates work best.)
◇ Crayons
◇ A pipe cleaner
◇ Construction paper
◇ A pencil
◇ A ruler
◇ Scissors
◇ Glue
◇ A stapler
◇ 2 paper fasteners

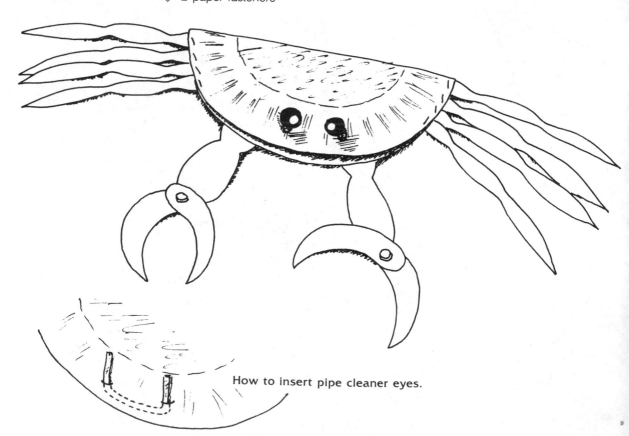

How to insert pipe cleaner eyes.

DIRECTIONS

Tell the children the following instructions: "Color the front and the back of the plate with crayons. Crabs come in many different colors, so it doesn't matter which color you choose. The easiest way to color the plate is to take the paper off a crayon and to color with the crayon on its side.

"Fold the plate in half with the bottom on the outside.

"To make the stalk eyes, use anything that is pointed to make two holes, 2 inches apart, in the front rim of the plate. Insert both ends of a pipe cleaner through these holes so the ends stick up. Use the pattern to trace two circle eyeballs onto construction paper. Cut them out. Bend one end of the pipe cleaner so it forms a little flat circle. Glue on a paper eyeball. Repeat with the other end of the pipe cleaner.

"Use the pattern to trace two front claws, two pincers, and eight legs onto construction paper. Cut out the pieces.

"Insert four legs in one side of the crab. Put them close together so they are touching each other. Staple them in the folded plate so the plate is fastened shut on the side. Staple the other four legs into the other side of the plate.

"Use a paper fastener to fasten a pincer to a front claw, by inserting the fastener in the dots on the pattern. Glue the claw under the front of the crab. Repeat with the other pincer and claw.

"Let the crab dry upside down or his claws will fall off."

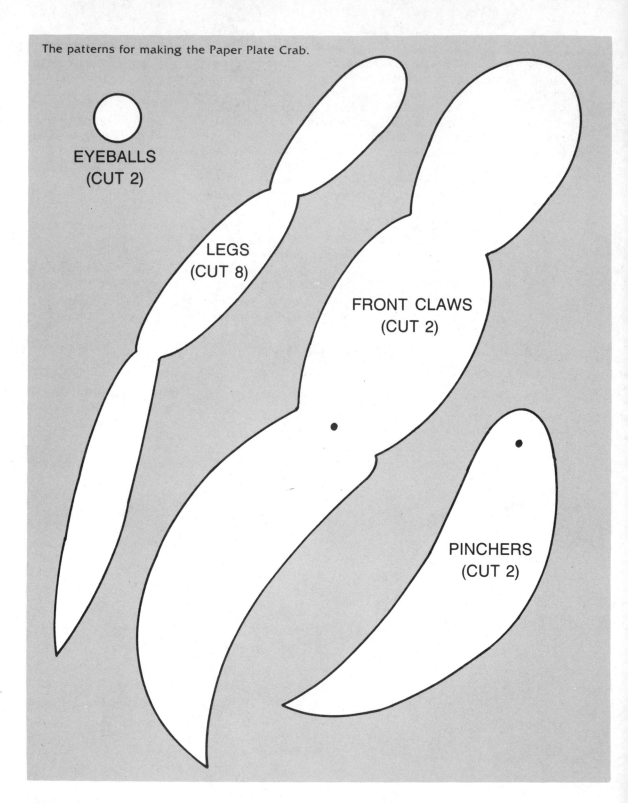

The patterns for making the Paper Plate Crab.

EYEBALLS
(CUT 2)

LEGS
(CUT 8)

FRONT CLAWS
(CUT 2)

PINCHERS
(CUT 2)

ALLIGATOR BREAD

Mix the dough 1½ hours before you want to bake it. This recipe makes enough dough for one large alligator.

AGE GROUP

Children of all ages will enjoy making Alligator Bread and letting him eat cookies before they eat him.

MATERIALS LIST

◇ A large bowl
◇ A wooden spoon
◇ A cookie sheet
◇ Aluminum foil
◇ ½ cup lukewarm milk
◇ 1 package active dry yeast
◇ ½ cup unseasoned mashed potato
◇ ¼ cup sugar

◇ ¼ cup margarine (½ stick), softened
◇ 1 egg
◇ ¾ teaspoon salt
◇ ¾ teaspoon pumpkin pie spice
◇ 2¼ cups flour
◇ ½ cup raisins
◇ Large cookies to feed the alligator
◇ Extra shortening and flour

DIRECTIONS

Help the children measure the lukewarm milk into the large bowl. Add the yeast and stir until dissolved.

Help the children measure and add the potato, sugar, margarine, egg, salt, pumpkin pie spice, flour, and raisins. They can take turns stirring the dough with the wooden spoon until it is mixed, or you can use an electric mixer with a dough hook and mix on slow speed for 2 minutes. If the children mix the dough by hand, lay it on a floured breadboard or countertop and let them take turns kneading it until it is smooth and elastic. Add extra flour if it gets sticky.

Put the dough in a greased bowl. Turn it over to grease the top. Cover the bowl with plastic wrap or a wet towel, and let the dough rise in a warm place (85° F) for 1½ hours.

Now the dough is ready to use. Put aprons on the children. Spread a little flour on the breadboard or countertop. The children can shape the dough into a long alligator with a pointed tail. Use a pizza cutter to cut off one-fourth of the alligator. Cut this piece into four equal pieces. These are the alligator's legs. Stick them on the alligator by pressing the dough together. Use a pair of scissors to cut the alligator's mouth open.

Make a round, flat "cookie" from aluminum foil. Grease the foil cookie on both sides with shortening. Stick it in the alligator's mouth to keep it open while he bakes.

Cover the alligator with "scales" made of raisins. Lay him on the greased cookie sheet. Bake in a preheated oven at 375° F for 20 minutes.

Remove Alligator Bread from the cookie sheet and take the foil out of his mouth. Put cookies in his mouth so part of them are sticking out. Eat him with butter.

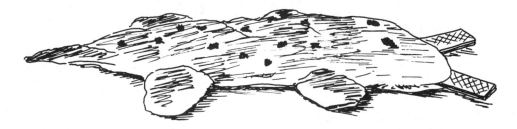

MAKING APPLESAUCE

Apples simmering on the stove make a home smell delicious.

AGE GROUP

Every child will enjoy peeling, cutting, mashing, and eating.

MATERIALS LIST

◇ 4 large apples
◇ 1 tablespoon water
◇ A 2-quart saucepan with lid
◇ A vegetable peeler
◇ A table knife
◇ A potato masher
◇ 2 tablespoons sugar

DIRECTIONS

Help the children peel the apples. They should cut each apple into fourths and remove the core with the table knife.

Put the apples in the saucepan. Add 1 tablespoon water. Cover the saucepan with its lid. Cook over high heat until the water begins to boil, about 1 minute. Reduce heat to low. Simmer the apples for 20 minutes until they are soft. Remove them from the heat.

Let the children mash the apples with the potato masher. They can add 2 tablespoons sugar and mash the apples some more. Eat the applesauce hot or cold.

SEPTEMBER
CRAFTS

A fter the older children have gone to school, you can enjoy some of the September crafts with the younger ones. You can also take a walk with them and pick up some of the signs of fall, for use with the Peek-A-Boo Picture.

PEEK-A-BOO PICTURE

Make a lovely picture with some signs of fall.

AGE GROUP

All ages will be able to create their own fall picture.

MATERIALS LIST

Each child needs:
◇ A pencil
◇ A ruler
◇ Scissors
◇ Glue
◇ Orange and yellow construction paper
◇ A tube of clear, household cement
  (Look in the Housewares department
  of grocery and drug stores.)
◇ A place to find some signs of fall
  (such as a park, a wooded yard,
  or a forest preserve.)

DIRECTIONS

Give the children the following instructions: "Use a pencil and ruler to draw a large X in the middle of a sheet of yellow construction paper (as shown in the pattern). Carefully cut on the X lines. The cuts form four triangles in the center of the paper. Starting at the tip, roll one of the triangles around the pencil to curl it. Remove the pencil and the curl will remain.

Repeat with the remaining triangles until all four are curled away from the center of the paper. Turn the paper over. Spread glue around its edges. Carefully glue it to the sheet of orange construction paper. This makes a curled frame for your signs of fall.

Take a walk outside and collect a few signs of fall, such as a red or yellow leaf, a small pine cone, an acorn, seeds, berries, pods, dry grasses, and fall flowers.

"Glue them inside your curled frame, using clear, household cement. Lay your Peek-A-Boo Picture flat and let it dry overnight."

A IS FOR APPLE

A pipe cleaner worm pops out to say that apple begins with A.

AGE GROUP

Children from ages 2 to 6 learn about the letter A as they make this picture from a circle, a rectangle, and two diamonds. They also practice writing, with your help.

MATERIALS LIST

Each child needs:
◇ Yellow, red, green, and white construction paper
◇ A pen
◇ A ruler
◇ Scissors
◇ Glue
◇ A paper punch
◇ Cellophane tape
◇ A pipe cleaner, cut in half
◇ A black marker

DIRECTIONS

Help your children use the ruler to draw a line across the top of the yellow construction paper. They can print *Aa is for Apple* on the line with a pen. If one of them needs your help, first make sure he is holding the pen correctly. Then lightly place your hand on top of his, and guide him in making the letters. As he writes with your help, tell him the name of each letter.

Use the pattern to trace a rectangle stem and two diamond leaves onto green construction paper. Trace the circle apple onto red paper. Make a hole in the apple with the paper punch.

Cut out these pieces. Encourage children 3 years old and up to do their own cutting.

The children should bend their pipe cleaner into a curly worm shape. Insert about half of the worm in the hole of the apple. Tape it in place.

Next have the children glue the circle apple, rectangle stem, and diamond leaves onto the yellow paper.

Make two eyes with the paper punch and white construction paper for each child. Let the children draw a dot on each eye with a black marker. They should put a drop of glue on the end of the worm. Then they can stick the eyes, slightly overlapping, on the glue.

Help each child write his name at the bottom of the page.

The "A is For Apple" picture.

Aa is for Apple

Barbara

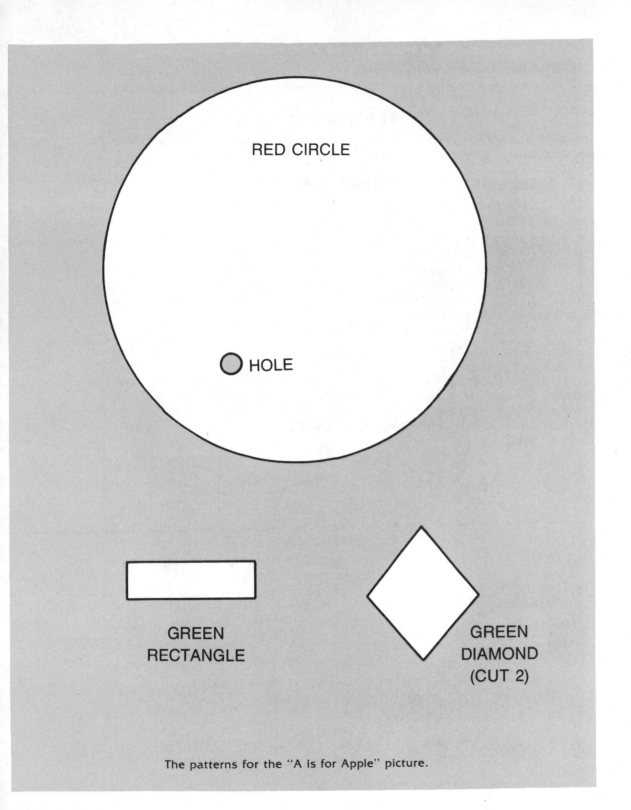

RED CIRCLE

HOLE

GREEN
RECTANGLE

GREEN
DIAMOND
(CUT 2)

The patterns for the "A is for Apple" picture.

CEREAL NECKLACE

Stringing small items onto a plastic needle is a fun way to practice making little fingers work, especially if the result is as good to eat as a Cereal Necklace.

AGE GROUP

This craft is especially designed for a child 2 years old and up to practice eye-hand coordination skills. Older children can make this necklace as a gift for younger friends.

MATERIALS LIST

Each child needs:
◇ A 26″ piece of clean, white string
◇ A large plastic needle (often found in the Sewing and Knitting Notions section of drug stores.)
◇ Fruit-flavored cereal, shaped like the letter **O**
◇ A roll of hard candy, shaped like the letter **O**
◇ Miniature marshmallows

DIRECTIONS

Tie the string onto the needle. Tie a piece of candy on the end of the string to keep everything from falling off. Pour small amounts of cereal, candy, and marshmallow into three bowls.

Tell each child to string these items by putting the needle through the center of each one. Show him how to alternate a piece of candy, a marshmallow, and a piece of cereal until the string is filled. Then remove the needle and tie the ends of the necklace together.

The children can wear the necklaces until they get hungry. Then they can nibble the goodies off the string.

SHAPES LOCOMOTIVE

This is a six-piece preschool puzzle. If you let the child do the work, he will gain valuable practice in tracing around a pattern, cutting, coloring, gluing, as well as putting the puzzle together.

AGE GROUP

Shapes Locomotive is especially for preschoolers from 2 to 5. Older children can make a set of cardboard tracing pieces as a gift for a younger friend. They could put the tracing set in a decorated envelope. Include a cotton ball for smoke, plus simple directions such as: Trace, Cut Out, Color, Make a Locomotive.

MATERIALS LIST

Each child needs:
◇ A pencil
◇ Cardboard for making a pattern
  (Poster board can be found in the
  School Supplies section of stores.)
◇ White and black construction paper
◇ Scissors
◇ Glue
◇ Crayons
◇ A cotton ball

DIRECTIONS

First, tell your child that a locomotive is the engine of the train, and that it pulls the other railroad cars.

Use the patterns to trace the parts of the locomotive onto cardboard. Cut these pieces out.

Give the child the four cardboard pieces. Help him use a pencil to trace around each piece onto white construction paper. He should trace three circle wheels, and one of everything else.

Help him cut out the locomotive pieces. He should arrange the pieces to look like a locomotive on a black sheet of paper.

Then he should color the locomotive pieces with crayon, perhaps adding a window for the engineer to look out. He should glue the pieces in place on the black paper, with cotton-ball smoke coming from the smokestack.

WOOLIE-PULLIE

Cut a Styrofoam egg carton in half. Pour poster paints in the six cups. Your child can paint with the brilliant hues without ruining the bottles by mixing colors.

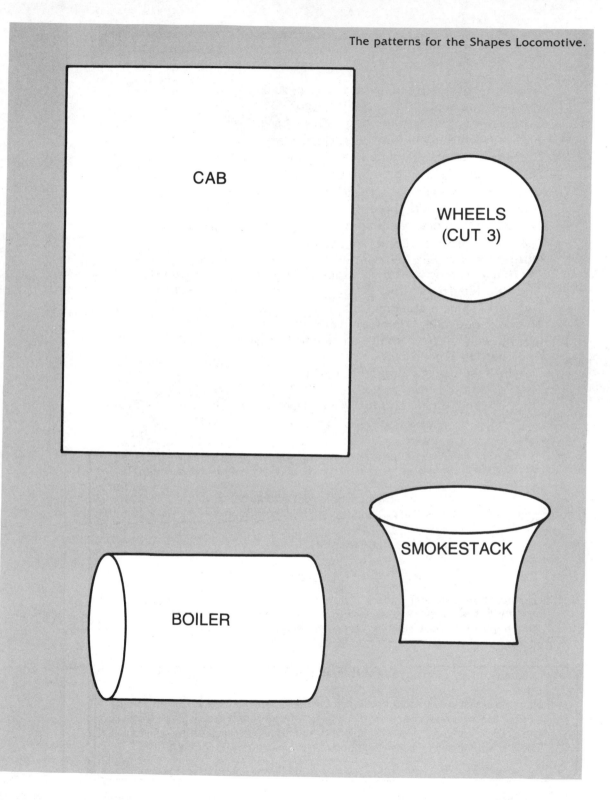

CAB

WHEELS
(CUT 3)

SMOKESTACK

BOILER

FINGERPRINT SPIDERS

Preschoolers will enjoy learning the following poem before making the spiders:

Five little spiders standing in a row. (Hold up 5 fingers.)
The first one said, "Come on. Let's go."
Out he went, through the door, (Swish 1 finger away.)
And that left spiders four. (Hold up 4 fingers.)
Four little spiders standing in a row. (Hold up 4 fingers.)
The next one said, "Come on. Let's go."
Out he went to climb a tree, (Make 1 finger climb an imaginary tree.)
And that left spiders three.
Three little spiders standing in a row. (Hold up 3 fingers.)
The next one said, "Come on. Let's go."
Out he went to see the zoo,
    (Curl fingers and thumb into a circle and look through circle with eye.)
And that left spiders two.
Two little spiders standing in a row. (2 fingers.)
The next one said, "Come on. Let's go."
Out he went to have some fun, (Make finger jump up and down.)
And that left spider one.
One little spider standing in a row. (1 finger.)
Then he said, "I have to go."
Out he went to play and run, (Swish finger back and forth.)
And that left spiders none. (Hold up fist.)

MATERIALS LIST

Each child needs:
◇ Construction paper in light colors
◇ A stamp pad (Look in the School Supplies
   section of stores.)
◇ A black marker

DIRECTIONS

Tell the children: "Press a finger onto the stamp pad, then press onto the construction paper.
"Repeat with five fingers on one hand. Then wash your hands with soap and water.
"Use the marker to draw eight legs on each spider. Add some eyes."

WOOLIE-PULLIE

To make a stamp pad, pour poster paint into a Styrofoam meat tray lined with
a paper towel. The towel helps the paint spread evenly and prevents splashes.
The children can use the following things as stamps: a carrot cut across, a cotton
ball, a toilet-paper roll, measuring cups turned upside down, cookie cutters.

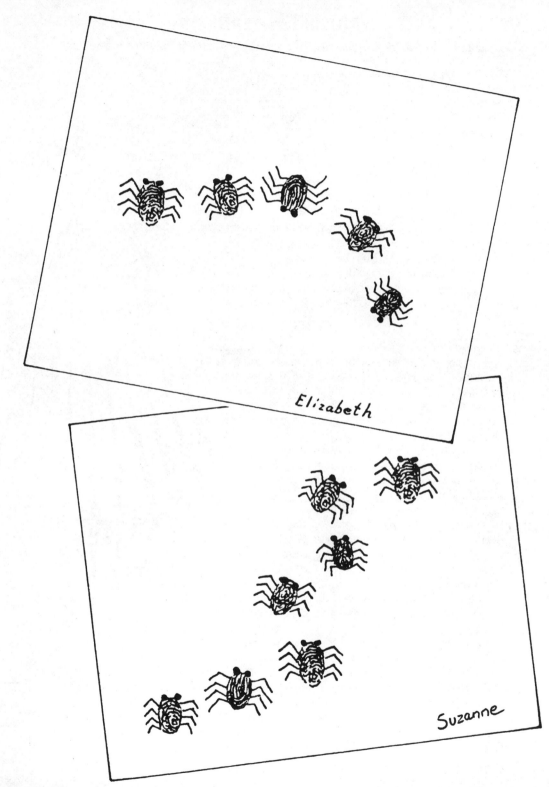

Elizabeth

Suzanne

PAPER LANTERN

Paper Lantern makes a pretty decoration for a backyard party or for someone's room.

AGE GROUP

This craft is for children from ages 4 to 10. Preschool children will learn to cut on lines and to match the shapes of the candle flames. Everyone will learn a new construction skill.

MATERIALS LIST

Each child needs:

◇ A pencil
◇ A ruler
◇ Red, yellow, and blue construction paper
◇ Scissors
◇ Glue
◇ A paper punch
◇ Ribbon, yarn, or string for hanging the lantern

DIRECTIONS

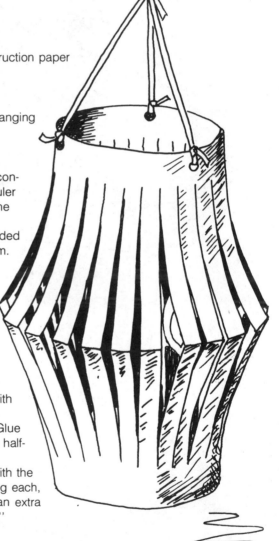

Instruct the children as follows: "Fold a sheet of red construction paper in half lengthwise. Use a pencil and ruler to draw three ½-inch cut lines every ½ inch along the folded edge. Cut on these lines.

"Open the paper. Curl it into a cylinder with the folded edge outward and the short ends at the top and bottom. This makes a lantern shape. Overlap the edge of the cylinder ¾ inch and glue it to hold its shape.

"Make candles by drawing four rectangles 1¼ × 3½ inches onto the blue construction paper. Cut them out.

"Use the pattern to draw eight large yellow flames and eight small red flames. Cut them out.

"Glue a yellow flame on each side of a candle, so the candle looks the same from both sides. Glue a red flame in the center of each yellow flame. Repeat with the remaining candles.

"Put the four candles upright inside the lantern. Glue them along the inside edge of the lantern, putting glue halfway up each candle. Let the lantern dry upside down.

"Make three holes around the top of the lantern with the paper punch. Tie three pieces of ribbon, 12 inches long each, in the holes. Tie the ribbons together at the top. Tie an extra piece of ribbon to the knot to hang up Paper Lantern."

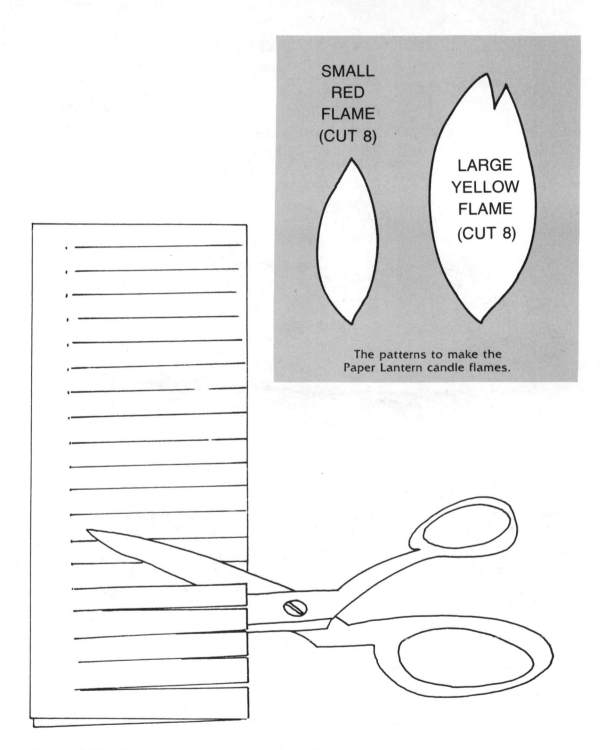

SMALL
RED
FLAME
(CUT 8)

LARGE
YELLOW
FLAME
(CUT 8)

The patterns to make the
Paper Lantern candle flames.

How to fold and cut the paper to make a Paper Lantern.

DOGS IN A BLANKET

Hot dog! These are fun to make and good to eat. Even your youngest child can help prepare lunch or supper with this recipe.

AGE GROUP

Dogs in a Blanket can be made and enjoyed by all children.

MATERIALS LIST

◇ 20 refrigerator biscuits in a can
◇ 10 hot dogs
◇ A cookie sheet
◇ Oil

DIRECTIONS

The children should spread a tiny bit of oil all over the cookie sheet. Then help them open the cans of refrigerator biscuits.

The children can take turns making the Dogs in a Blanket. Have one lay two biscuits on the cookie sheet, with one slightly overlapping the other. He should lay a hot dog longways on the biscuits. Then he can pinch the biscuit up around the hot dog, covering all of it but the ends.

Turn the pinched side over so it rests on the pan to keep it from unwrapping as it bakes. Repeat with the other hot dogs.

Bake in a preheated oven at 400° F for 15 minutes, or until the biscuits are nice and brown. Dip in catsup or mustard and eat.

GRANOLA AND CELERY BITS

These snacks are crunchy and delicious; easy and nutritious!

AGE GROUP

All ages, including Moms and Dads, love this snack. Children 2 years old and up learn to follow directions, and to cut and spread with a table knife.

MATERIALS LIST

◇ Several stalks of celery
◇ Peanut butter
◇ Granola or "natural cereal" that looks like granola
◇ A knife for spreading
◇ A knife for cutting (For use with adult supervision.)
◇ A cutting board

DIRECTIONS

Wash the celery in cold water. Dry it with a towel. Cut off both ends to get rid of brown spots.

Have the children use the spreading knife to fill each stalk with peanut butter. They should lay the filled celery on the cutting board. You should help them cut it into ½-inch pieces.

Pour granola into a bowl. Have the children roll each celery bit in the granola and arrange them on a plate. They can eat them and share some, too.

OCTOBER
CRAFTS

When Halloween was close by, I visited my daughter's third-grade classroom to help children make Sweet-Gum Spiders. Several days later I received thank-you notes from the children. The spelling and words are theirs.

Dear Mrs. Dondiego,
    Thank you for the art project. I think it is sooooo cute! We hung him on the fan in the kitchen. When we would turn on the fan the little spider would go nuts! And my step Dad Mark is so tall that he would walk right under it, and it would cetch on his hair.

                        Love, Christy

Dear Mrs. Dondiego,
    Thank you for coming and helping us with the spiders. I hope you dress up as a turkey for Thanksgiving.

                        Sincerely, Brad

Dear Mrs. Dondiego,

That art project was fun. I had to put it in my room. I named it Fanky. Fanky wasn't very happy. He didn't have fun spinning a web in the door. I love you.

Fondly, Peter

Dear Mrs. Dondiego,

Thankyouforcommingtoteachmeandmyfriendshowtodothespider. Ilikeddoingitwithyoualot. Thepartllikedbestiswhenlhadtodothelegs.

Sincerely, Dianna

Dear Mrs. Dondiego,

Thank you for coming and helping us make a spider. Even thow my mom threw it away I still liked it.

Sincerely, Alex

SWEET-GUM SPIDER

The sweet gum is a shade tree found in the Eastern United States. Its seed pod, a dark brown spiny ball called a *gum ball*, makes a wonderful prickly spider. Best of all, gum balls are free.

AGE GROUP

This project will interest all children as a useful decoration. It provides good practice in eye-hand coordination for preschoolers.

MATERIALS LIST

Each child needs:
◇ A plastic cap from a milk bottle
◇ A pencil
◇ A ruler
◇ Scissors
◇ Glue
◇ Black and white construction paper
◇ A gum ball with a stem, from the sweet gum tree
◇ Eight 6″ pipe cleaners (From the Smoking section of a drugstore.)
◇ Black thread
◇ Black spray paint (From the Hardware or Craft section of a drugstore.)
◇ A paper punch

DIRECTIONS

Instruct the children as follows: "Use the pencil to trace around a plastic cap from a milk bottle, making a circle on black construction paper. The circle will have a diameter of about 1¾ inches. Cut out the circle.

"Use the ruler to measure and draw a rectangle 1½ x 3½ inches on black paper. Cut out the rectangle.

"Fold the circle in half. Starting in the middle of the folded edge, make a ½-inch cut, straight up. Don't cut the circle in half! Open the circle. Fold it in half again, but this time fold it on the cut. Again starting in the middle of the folded edge, make a ½-inch cut, straight up. When you open the circle, the two cuts should make a plus sign in the middle of it. This is the hat brim.

"The cuts form four triangles in the center of the hat brim. Bend the triangles upward. Apply glue to the outside of each triangle.

"Roll the black rectangle into a cylinder 1½ inches tall. Overlap the sides ½ inch and glue to make it hold its shape. Slip this cylinder over the four triangles of the hat brim.

"Use your fingers to press the triangles against the inside of the cylinder. The triangles will try to come loose, but just keep pressing on each one until the glue begins to dry and stick. Set the hat aside while you make the spider.

"Put a small amount of glue in the plastic milk cap. It is now your glue container. Dip one end of a pipe cleaner into the glue and insert it in one of the holes of the gum ball. Repeat with all eight pipe cleaners, inserting four pipe cleaners in one side of the gum ball, in as straight a line as possible, and four pipe cleaners in the other side. Leave room on the "face" of the spider for its eyes.

"Bend each pipe cleaner leg in half, then bend a small foot at the end. Tie a 20-inch piece of black thread to the gum ball's stem. This is the spider's web.

"Slip the hat over the thread and the stem.

"Use the black spray paint to paint the spider, hat and all. Do this out-of-doors or in a well-ventilated area, and use newspapers to keep other things from getting painted. Hold the spider by the thread when painting, flipping and turning it to paint the entire thing black. (An adult should do the painting, but the children will enjoy watching.)

After the paint dries, tell the children: "Glue on two white circle eyes made from construction paper. Add two black circle eyeballs made with the paper punch from construction paper.

"Hang the spider up in a doorway where he can catch in people's hair."

THE *MAYFLOWER*

This famous sailing ship carried the Pilgrims from England to Plymouth, Massachusetts, in 1620. In 1621, the Pilgrims held a harvest festival, giving thanks to God for their friends, their homes, and their food. It was the first Thanksgiving.

AGE GROUP

Children from ages 2 to 8 will be interested in the *Mayflower*. Preschoolers can practice cutting, gluing, drawing, and writing their name.

MATERIALS LIST

Each child needs:
◇ A black marker
◇ A ruler
◇ Blue, white, and yellow construction paper
◇ Scissors
◇ Glue
◇ A 6″ piece of yarn
◇ Tape
◇ A cotton ball

DIRECTIONS

The *Mayflower* is made of two triangles. One triangle is cut into three pieces to make the sails and flag. The other triangle is cut into two pieces to make the hull of the boat and the anchor. Instruct the children as follows:

"Use the ruler to draw a black line down the middle of the blue construction paper. This is the mast.

"Use the pattern to draw a triangle on white construction paper. Cut out the triangle, then cut the triangle into three equal sections (as shown on the pattern). Turn the top of the triangle sideways and glue it to the top of the mast to make a flag. Glue the other two pieces on the mast with a little space between them so they look like sails.

"Use the hull pattern to draw a triangle on yellow paper. Cut it out. Cut a 1½-inch tip from the triangle (as shown on the pattern) to make an anchor. Glue the hull below the sails.

"To attach the anchor, glue one end of the yarn under the hull. Tape the other end onto the anchor. The anchor should dangle below the picture.

"Use the black marker to draw a few waves near the ship. Draw seagulls flying in the sky. Print your name on the flag. Spread a little glue in the sky and stick on wisps of cotton for clouds."

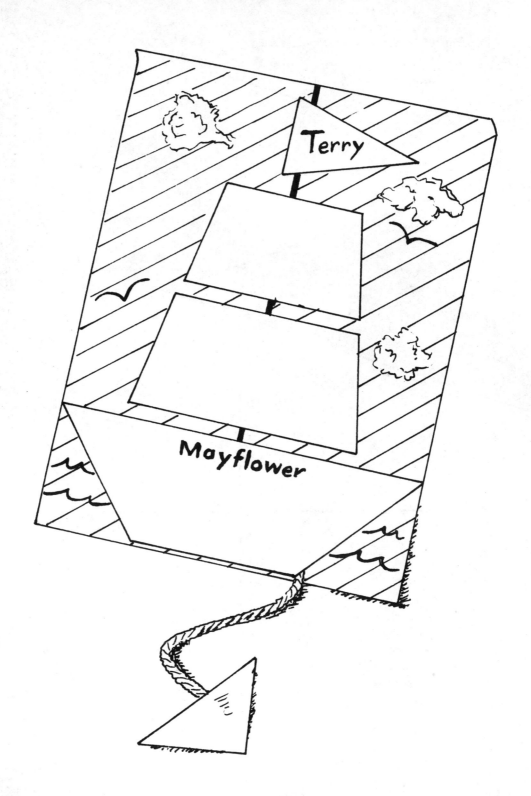

The pattern to make The *Mayflower's* sails.

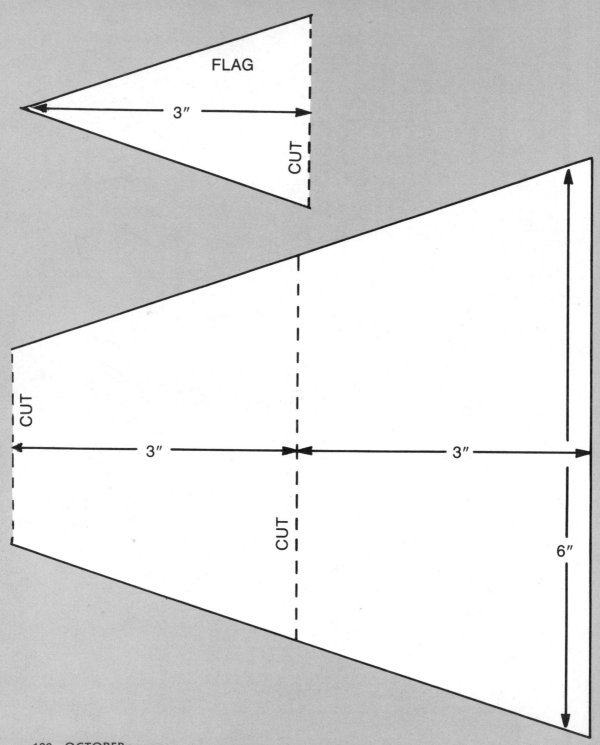

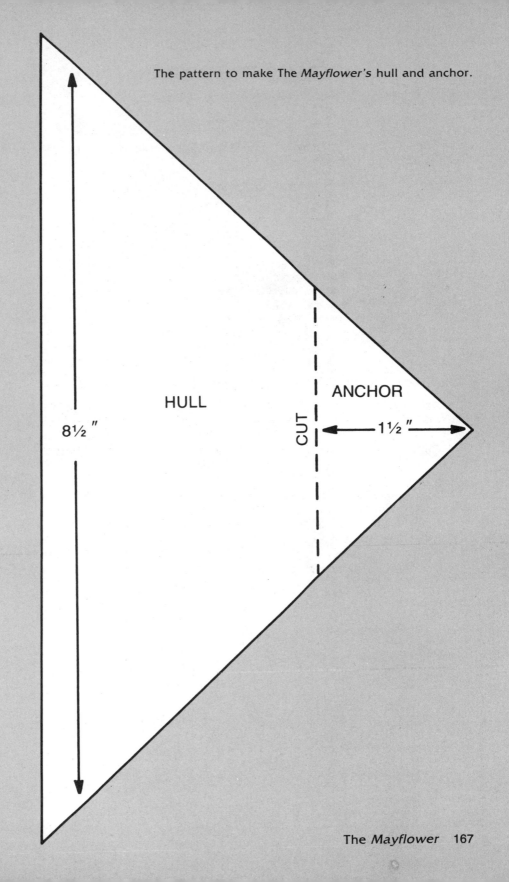

The pattern to make The *Mayflower's* hull and anchor.

HULL

ANCHOR

CUT

8½ "

1½ "

PAPER-PLATE WITCH

This witch will really grab you!

AGE GROUP

Children from ages 2 to 8 will enjoy making the witch as they learn about shapes. She is made from three triangles, a rectangle, and a circle.

MATERIALS LIST

Each child needs:
◇ A pencil
◇ A ruler
◇ Scissors
◇ Glue
◇ Black construction paper
◇ A black marker
◇ Green, yellow, and black crayons
◇ 9″ paper plate (Cheap generic plates work best.)
◇ A stapler

DIRECTIONS

Give the following directions to the children: "Use the patterns to trace three triangles onto black construction paper. Cut them out. Measure and cut out a black rectangle ½ x 9 inches for the hat brim.

"Cut the middle from the paper plate, leaving the rim in one piece. The circle from the middle of the plate is the witch's head. The rim will be her arms.

"Color the head green or yellow with crayon. To make hair, snip the edges of the two hair triangles to fringe them (as shown on the pattern). Glue one on each side of her face. Wrinkle the ends of her hair.

"Glue the hat triangle on her head. Add the hat brim. Draw a scary face with a black marker. Be sure to add a wart to the witch's nose.

"To make fingers, snip triangle pieces from the two ends of the plate rim. Color the fingers green or yellow. Color the rest of the rim black for arms.

"Staple the head onto the arms. Then make your witch grab someone!"

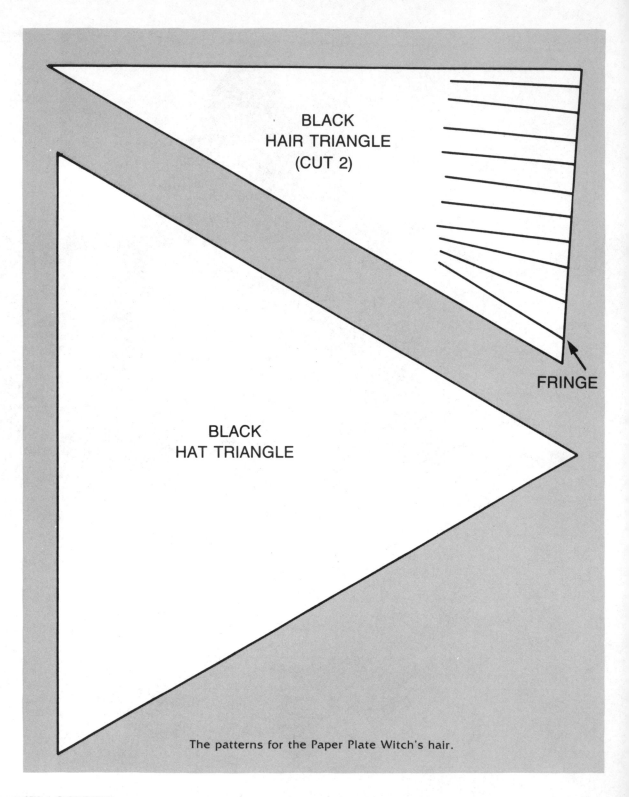

BLACK
HAIR TRIANGLE
(CUT 2)

FRINGE

BLACK
HAT TRIANGLE

The patterns for the Paper Plate Witch's hair.

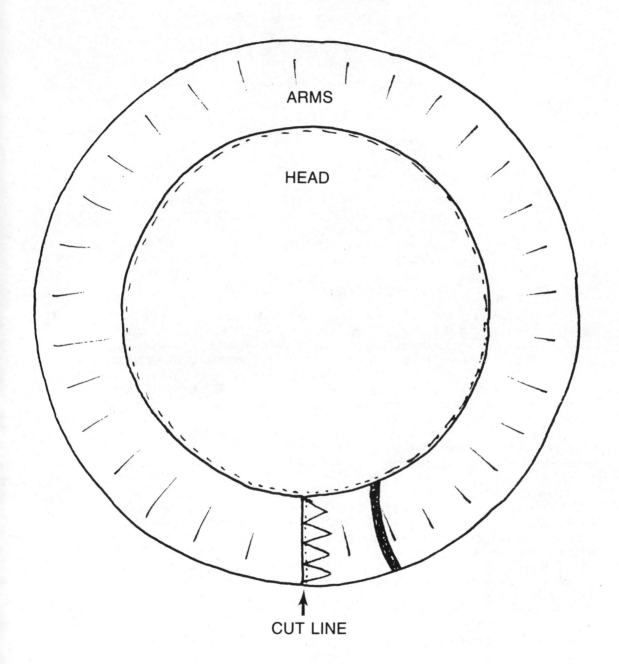

ARMS

HEAD

CUT LINE

How to cut the paper plate to make the Paper Plate Witch.

CONE WITCH

Children can make a witchy table decoration as they learn to put together triangles, rectangles, circles, and a cone.

AGE GROUP

This craft will challenge children 8 years old and up.

MATERIALS LIST

Each child needs:
◇ A pencil
◇ A ruler
◇ Scissors
◇ Glue
◇ Black, orange, and green construction paper
◇ Black and red markers
◇ A pipe cleaner (Look in the Tobacco section of drugstores.)

DIRECTIONS

Instruct the children as follows: "Fold a sheet of black construction paper in half crosswise. Lay the cone-shaped pattern on the fold. Trace and cut out through both papers, but do not cut on the fold. Open the cone shape. Hold it at each point with the flat edge at the top. Pull your hands together and downward. Overlap the edges until the paper comes to a point at the top. Glue the cone to make it hold its shape. Set it aside to dry.

"Use the pattern to trace a black triangle for the hat, two black triangles for the feet, and two smaller black triangles for the hair. Cut out the pieces. Fringe the hair (as shown on the pattern).

"Use the pattern to draw a circle face on green paper. Cut out the face. Glue one hair triangle on each side of the face. Glue a triangle hat on the top of the witch's head. Draw a rectangle ½ x 3 inches on black paper. Cut it out. This is the hat brim. Glue it on the base of the hat.

"Draw eyes, eyebrows, and a nose with a black marker. Draw a mouth with a red marker.

"Bend one end of the pipe cleaner into a circle slightly smaller than the witch's head. Twist the pipe cleaner onto itself so it will hold its circle shape. Spread glue on the pipe cleaner circle. Press the head on so that the straight end of the pipe cleaner makes a neck for the witch. Insert the neck into the top of the cone body. Add a drop of glue to hold the neck in place.

"Measure a rectangle ½ x 7 inches on black construction paper for the arms. Cut it out and wrap it around the cone body near the top so that the arms stick out in front of the witch. Glue in place.

"Measure a broomstick ¼ x 6 inches on black paper. Cut it out and glue it to the end of one arm.

"Measure a rectangle 1 x 1½ inches on orange construction paper for the broom straws. Cut it out and snip the edges to fringe them. Glue the rectangle onto the end of the broomstick. Add a little strip of black paper at the top of the fringes or draw a black line across the broomstraws.

"Glue two triangle feet inside the front hem of the witch's dress. Fold them so they point toward the front. Your Cone Witch is ready for Halloween!

Cone Witch 173

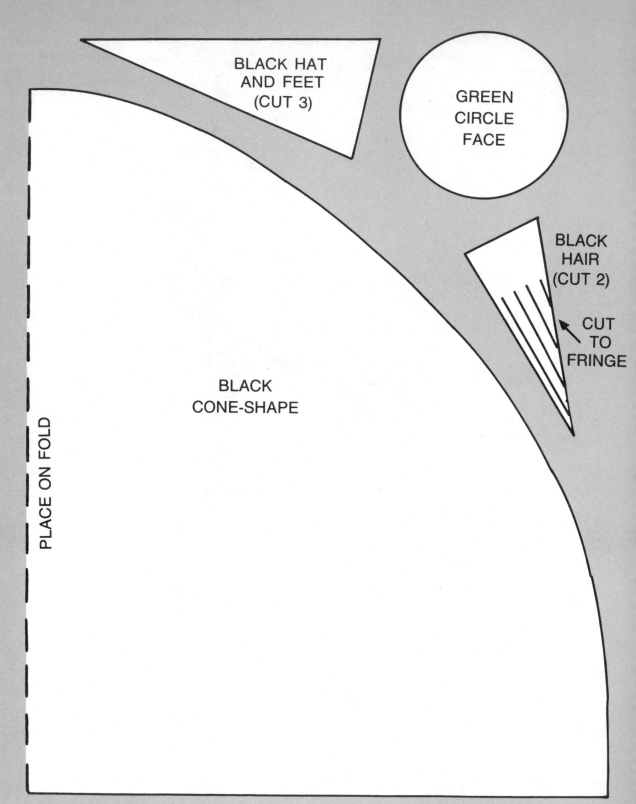

BLACK HAT
AND FEET
(CUT 3)

GREEN
CIRCLE
FACE

BLACK
HAIR
(CUT 2)

CUT
TO
FRINGE

BLACK
CONE-SHAPE

PLACE ON FOLD

The patterns to make a Cone Witch.

MAKING A QUILL PEN AND INVISIBLE INK

A *quill* is a large feather from the wing or tail of a bird. It was used for writing from the sixth century until the middle of the nineteenth century. Children can make their own quill pens, and then write secret, invisible messages.

AGE GROUP

This craft is suitable for children 6 years old and up.

MATERIALS LIST

For each child you need:
◇ A feather, the larger, the better (Look in a craft store.)
◇ Sharp scissors
◇ A toothpick
◇ A lemon, or bottled lemon juice
◇ White paper
You also need a lamp with a removable shade

DIRECTIONS

Use scissors to snip the tip off the quill. Use a toothpick to hollow it out. Pour lemon juice into a small container. Tell the children to dip the quill pen into the juice and write a message on white paper. When the message dries, it will be invisible.

To make the invisible message appear, remove the shade from a lamp and turn it on. Let the children hold the paper against the light bulb. In a few minutes the message will appear in light brown letters.

Try making invisible ink from egg white mixed with water, and from sugar dissolved in water.

POP-UP PUMPKIN

A ghost is hiding in the pumpkin! Make this card to keep or to give away.

AGE GROUP

This is a good craft for all ages. Preschoolers will practice cutting, gluing, and writing skills.

MATERIALS LIST

Each child needs:
◇ A pencil
◇ A ruler
◇ A black marker
◇ Scissors
◇ Glue
◇ Orange, green, and white construction paper

DIRECTIONS

Instruct the children as follows: "To make the pumpkin, fold a sheet of orange construction paper in half crosswise. Place the bottom of the pumpkin pattern on the fold. Trace around it. Cut out through both papers, but do not cut the fold.

"Apply a thin line of glue to the left side of the pumpkin to seal it." The pattern shows where to glue. Help small children with this step to prevent them from using too much glue. Then tell the children:

"Measure and cut out two green strips, ¼ × 7 inches each. Curl them by wrapping them tightly around a pencil. These are pumpkin vines. Glue them on the top of the pumpkin (as shown on the pattern).

"Use the pattern to trace a stem onto green paper. Cut it out and glue it on the pumpkin. Draw lines on the pumpkin with a black marker so it will not look like an orange.

"Use the pattern to trace the ghost onto white construction paper. Cut it out. Draw black eyes and mouth with a marker. Write a message on the ghost, such as: HAPPY HALLOWEEN! or HAVE A BOO-TIFUL HALLOWEEN!

"Insert the ghost in the right side of the pumpkin. He will be hidden so that only the top of his head sticks out. Give Pop-Up Pumpkin to someone you like."

WOOLIE-PULLIE
Let the children paint with cotton-tipped swabs
instead of brushes for fast and easy cleanup.

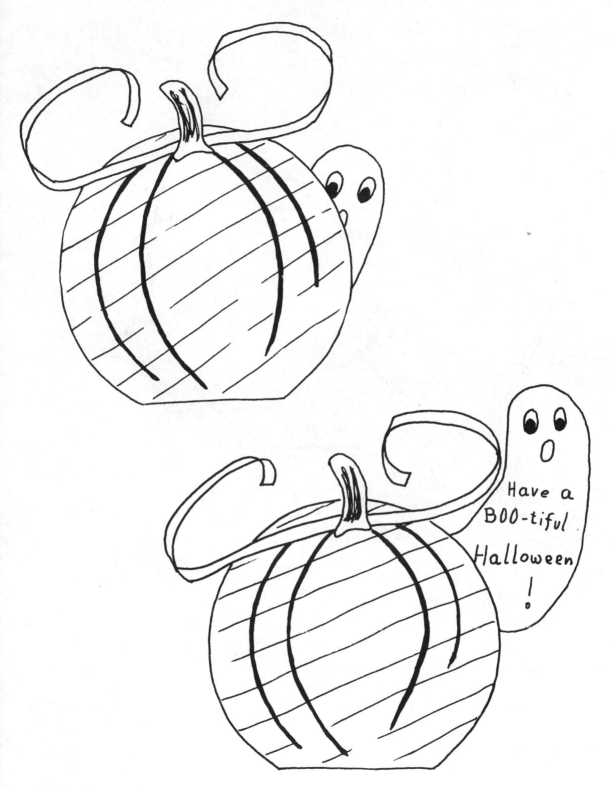

Have a
BOO-tiful

Halloween
!

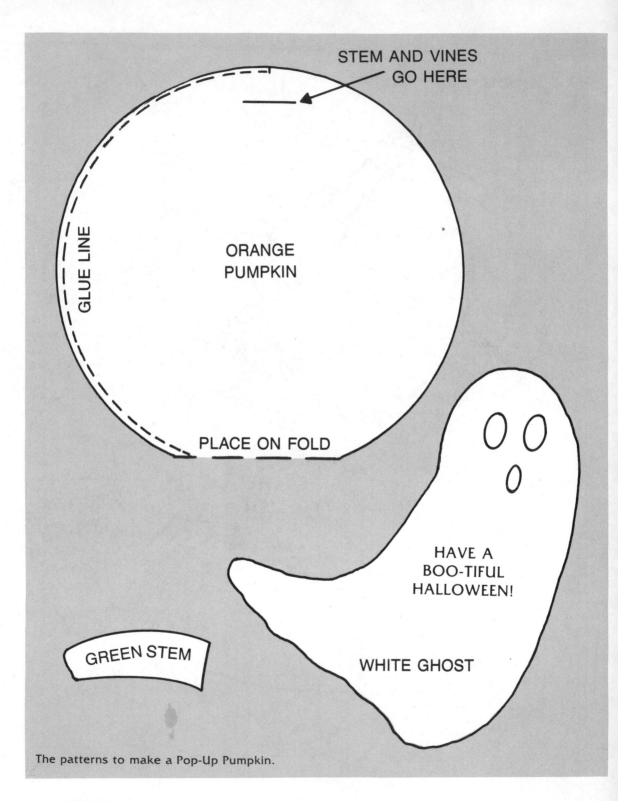

STEM AND VINES GO HERE

GLUE LINE

ORANGE PUMPKIN

PLACE ON FOLD

GREEN STEM

HAVE A BOO-TIFUL HALLOWEEN!

WHITE GHOST

The patterns to make a Pop-Up Pumpkin.

CYLINDER CAT

At our house we never throw away empty toilet-paper rolls. We transform them into crafts, or our gerbil chews them to bits to make a nest. Combine the roll with a circle, two rectangles, and two triangles to make a perfect pet for Cone Witch.

AGE GROUP

Because of the small pieces used to make Cylinder Cat, it is a good craft for children 8 years old and up.

MATERIALS LIST

Each child needs:
◇ A toilet-paper roll
◇ A pencil
◇ A ruler
◇ Scissors
◇ Glue
◇ Black, orange, and white construction paper
◇ A green marker

DIRECTIONS

Tell the children: "Cut an end off the toilet-paper roll so the roll is 3 inches long.

"Use the pencil and ruler to measure a rectangle 3 x 6 inches on black construction paper. Cut out the rectangle and spread glue on it. Wrap it around the roll to cover it. This is the cat's body.

"Measure two strips ¾ x 7½ inches on black paper. Cut them out. To make the cat's legs, drape one strip over the body, at the back of the roll. Glue the middle of the strip onto the body so that the two ends hang down evenly, forming the legs. Drape the second strip over the body, about ¾ inch back from the cat's head. Once again, glue the middle of the strip onto the body so that the ends hang down evenly. Fold the end of each leg outward ½ inch to make paws.

"Use the pattern to trace a circle face, two triangle ears, and a tail onto black construction paper. Cut out the pieces. Cut out two white eyes, an orange nose, and an orange mouth of your own design. Draw eyeballs on the eyes with a green marker. Cut out six skinny whiskers, each 2 inches long, from black construction paper.

"Glue the eyes, nose, mouth, and whiskers on the face. Glue the ears on the back of the face so they stick up.

"Apply glue to the front edge of the cat's body. Gently press the face onto the glue to make it stick to the end of the cylinder.

"Finish the Cylinder Cat by gluing the tail inside the top of the roll. Curl the tail a little by wrapping it around your finger."

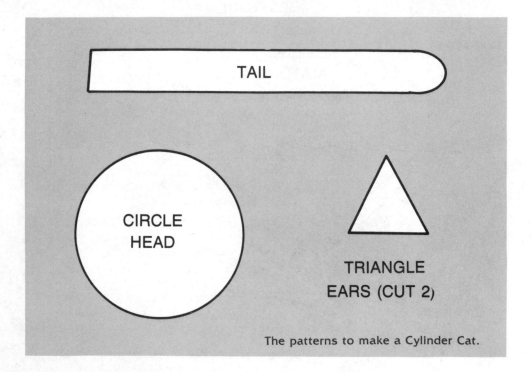

The patterns to make a Cylinder Cat.

POPCORN BALLS

Children can color these treats by adding food dye to the syrup.

AGE GROUP

All children will enjoy making Popcorn Balls. Be sure to remove any unpopped kernels from the corn.

MATERIALS LIST

◇ A large bowl or baking pan
◇ Solid shortening
◇ A 2-quart saucepan
◇ A wooden spoon
◇ 10 cups popped corn
◇ 1 cup sugar
◇ ⅓ cup water
◇ ⅓ cup molasses
◇ ¼ cup margarine (½ stick)
◇ 1 teaspoon salt
◇ 1 teaspoon vanilla
◇ Food coloring (optional)

DIRECTIONS

The children can grease the large bowl or pan, using their fingers and solid shortening. Then they can measure the popped corn into the pan. Preschoolers can practice counting to ten as the corn is measured.

Help them measure the sugar, water, molasses, margarine, and salt into the saucepan. Now an adult must take over to prevent burns.

Cook this mixture over medium heat, stirring occasionally, until the sugar dissolves. Turn the heat to high and let the syrup come to a boil. Test it for doneness by dropping a small amount of syrup into a cup of cold water. The syrup will form a ball of candy in the bottom of the cup. Touch this ball with your finger. When the syrup is ready to use, it will form a hard ball in the cup of cold water. Continue testing the syrup as it cooks, until it reaches this hard-ball stage.

Remove the syrup from the heat. Add the vanilla and the food coloring. Stir. Pour the hot syrup over the popped corn. The children can stir the corn with wooden spoons until each piece is coated. The syrup is very hot, so they must not touch it.

Give each child a small piece of shortening. Tell them to coat their hands with it. They can pick up the coated corn and shape it into balls the size of a baseball. The shortening will help prevent the syrup from burning them because it does not let the popcorn stick to their hands.

This recipe makes about ten Popcorn Balls.

CARAMEL CORN

With this recipe, children learn that the very best foods are made in the kitchen, not bought in a box at the store.

AGE GROUP

Any child can help an adult make this recipe. All will enjoy eating it.

MATERIALS LIST

◇ A jelly-roll pan or large baking pan
◇ Solid shortening
◇ A 2-quart saucepan
◇ A wooden spoon
◇ 12 cups popped corn
◇ 2 cups cocktail peanuts
◇ 1⅓ cups sugar
◇ 1 cup (2 sticks) margarine
◇ ½ cup light corn syrup

DIRECTIONS

The children can grease the jelly-roll pan, using their fingers and solid shortening. Then they can mix the popped corn and the peanuts together in the pan. This is a good time to practice counting to 12 as the corn is measured.

Help them measure the sugar, margarine, and corn syrup into the saucepan. Now an adult must take over to prevent burns. Cook this mixture over medium heat, stirring occasionally, until it begins to boil.

Let it boil until it turns a light caramel color, about 10 minutes. Remove from the heat.

Pour the mixture over the popped corn and peanuts, letting the children stir with a wooden spoon to coat the pieces. Spread the coated corn and peanuts out in the pan to cool.

Break the Caramel Corn into pieces. Store it in a tightly covered container so it won't get sticky.

NOVEMBER
CRAFTS

This chapter includes four turkey crafts. My favorite third-grade class made Turkey Jars just before Thanksgiving. Their teacher and I filled the jars with gumdrops and told the children to offer their candy to their holiday guests at home instead of eating it themselves. Here are more letters, written the following week.

Dear Mrs. Dondiego,
I liked the turkey. My mom and dad did to. They liked the little eyes. I liked the mouth. It looked funny. I liked it all if you want the truth. Bye.

From, Peter G.

Dear Mrs. Dondiego,
I brought my turkey down to my grandma's house, but I lift it there. So when they come up for Chrismas they will bring it back. We left it on the table all the time we were there. We didn't wont it to get dirty so when we ate we didn't put it on the table.

Love, Peter T.

Dear Mommy,
Thank you for coming to my class. I think every one likes you coming to help. I do too. I realy liked making the turkey. I wish you came in every day for art. That would be real fun! The turkey was fun to make, but not to easy. If you didn't come we wouldn't be able to make it as good, probely not at all. Thank you for coming. I realy like you coming. I got to go my hand's getting tired.

Love, Elizabeth

TURKEY JAR FOR NUTS OR MINTS

To make this turkey with children under the age of 5, make the cone before beginning the craft. To speed up the project, cut the construction paper beforehand. Just remember: the more work you do, the less the child learns to do for himself.

AGE GROUP

With adult help, children as young as two can make the Turkey Jar. Children 6 years old and up can do their own tracing, measuring, and cutting with a little help from you.

MATERIALS LIST

You can buy the first three items in a craft store. Each child needs:
◇ Feathers (Use marabou craft feathers or any others)
◇ Red felt
◇ 2 paste-on movable eyes, size 3MM
◇ An empty 4½-oz baby-food jar, with lid
◇ A pencil
◇ A ruler
◇ Yellow, brown, and orange construction paper
◇ Glue
◇ Scissors that can cut the red felt
◇ A plastic cap from a milk bottle

DIRECTIONS

Instruct the children as follows: "Use the pencil and ruler to draw a rectangle 2¼ x 8½ inches on yellow construction paper. Cut it out. Apply glue to the rectangle and wrap it around the baby-food jar. It will cover the jar completely.

"Remove the lid from the jar. Trace around the lid on yellow construction paper to make a circle. Cut this out and glue it on the top of the lid. Set the lid aside until you are finished with your Turkey Jar, or it will get in your way.

"Use the patterns to trace the cone and two wings on brown construction paper. Trace two feet on orange construction paper. Trace the wattle on red felt. Cut out these pieces.

"To form the cone, hold the cone cutout with the flat edge at the top. Holding it at each point, pull your two hands together and downward. Overlap the edges until the paper comes to a sharp point at the top. Glue the cone to make it hold its shape.

"Draw three 2-inch slits straight up from the base of the cone; space them equally apart. Cut the slits and spread them out to form three tabs. Cut off one of the tabs and glue it to the jar to form the turkey's tail. Glue it with the wide part up, extending over the top of the jar. You will stick feathers behind it when we get to that step.

"Apply glue to the two tabs on the cone. Stick the cone on the front of the Turkey Jar, with the two tabs aimed down over the turkey's breast. The flat side of the cone, where the tab was cut off, is the top of the turkey's head.

"Glue a wing on each side of the jar. Glue two orange feet on the front of the turkey, near the bottom.

"Squirt some glue in the plastic cap from a milk bottle. Dip the end of each feather in the glue and insert it between the paper tail and the glass jar. Add a small feather to each paper wing. The turkey in the picture was made with seven feathers.

"Add the red felt wattle by applying glue to the felt and folding it over the tip of the cone beak. Glue on two movable eyes.

"Let the glue dry several hours. Then fill the jar with mints or peanuts. Put the lid on."

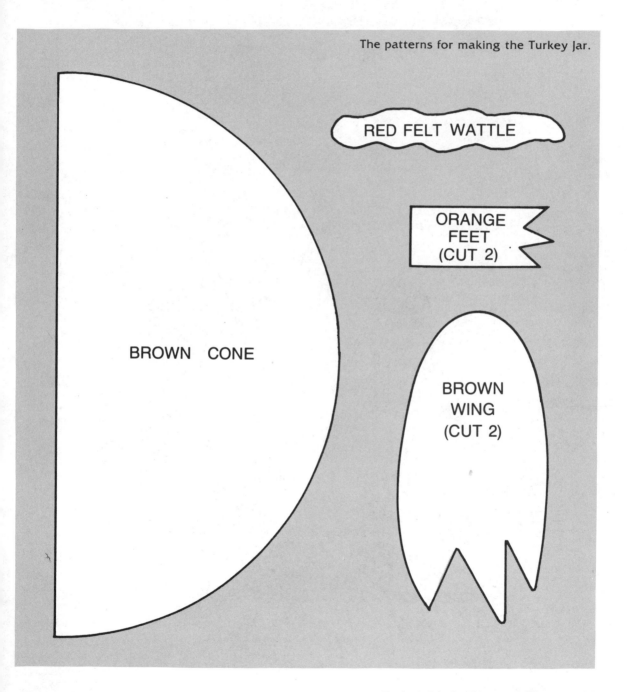

The patterns for making the Turkey Jar.

RED FELT WATTLE

ORANGE
FEET
(CUT 2)

BROWN CONE

BROWN
WING
(CUT 2)

HANG-UP TURKEY

Hang-Up Turkey helps us remember the things we are thankful for. He is made from a cone, giving children experience in using geometric shapes.

AGE GROUP

Preschoolers can make the turkey with adult help. It will interest all children through age 10.

MATERIALS LIST

Each child needs:
◇ A pencil
◇ A ruler
◇ Scissors
◇ Glue
◇ Yellow, red, and orange construction paper
◇ A sheet of yellow construction paper, 9 × 12 inches
◇ A black pen or marker
◇ Crayons
◇ A paper punch
◇ Ribbon or yarn, 24 inches long

DIRECTIONS

Give the children the following directions: "Use the patterns to trace a wattle onto red construction paper, a circle and two feet onto orange paper, and two wings onto yellow paper. Cut out the pieces.

"On the orange circle, print: *I AM THANKFUL FOR* _____. Set this aside.

"To make the turkey's cone, hold the sheet of yellow construction paper horizontally by its two top corners. Pull your two hands together and downward, overlapping the edges until the paper comes to a sharp point at the top. The sharp point is the turkey's beak. Glue the cone to make it hold its shape.

"Starting at the open base of the cone, cut toward the cone tip to make about 12 feathers. Each feather is 1 to 1½ inches wide. Leave 4½ inches of the cone tip uncut. Spread the feathers out by folding them at right angles to the cone.

"Trim the ends of the feathers so they are pointed. Color each feather with crayons in bright colors.

"Glue the circle that says, '*I AM THANKFUL FOR* _____,' to the back of the turkey. This will help hold his feathers up. On the back of each feather, write some things you are thankful for. They might include: *my family, my home, food, friends, my school, my teachers, my church, clothes,* and other things.

"Use the paper punch to make a hole in the top of the orange circle. Insert the piece of yarn or ribbon and tie the ends together so the turkey can be hung up.

"Use the black pen or marker to draw lines on the two orange feet. Glue the feet on top of two feathers at the bottom of the turkey.

"Color the wings with crayons. Glue one on each side of the turkey. Put glue on one end of the red wattle. Wrap the glued end over the tip of the cone, letting most of the wattle hang down. Leave some of the tip sticking out since this is the turkey's beak. Use a pen or marker to draw two eyes and nose holes.

"Hang up the turkey where you can see both sides of him."

How to cut the paper cone to make the Hang-Up Turkey.

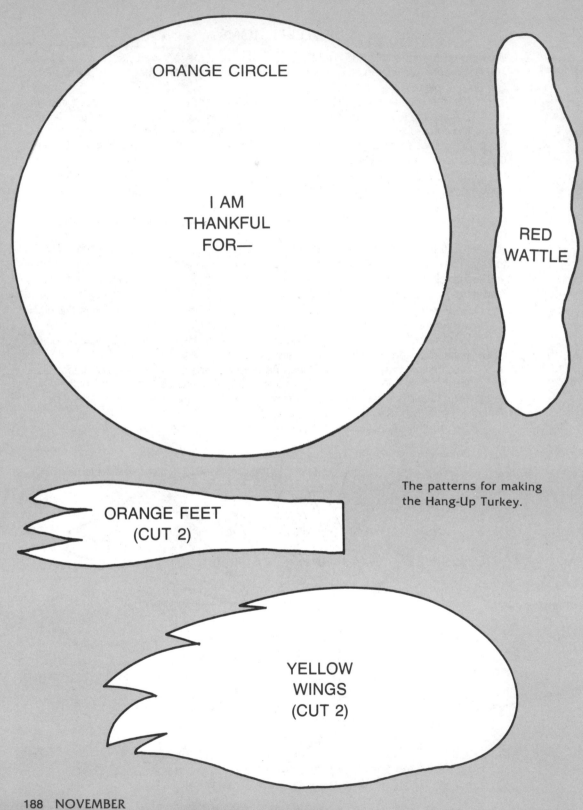

ORANGE CIRCLE

I AM
THANKFUL
FOR—

RED
WATTLE

The patterns for making
the Hang-Up Turkey.

ORANGE FEET
(CUT 2)

YELLOW
WINGS
(CUT 2)

TURKEY WITH CARTOON FEATHERS

Colorful cartoons from the Sunday funnies become bright feathers for a turkey.

AGE GROUP

Children as young as 2 years can learn to follow directions to create a turkey if an adult cuts out the pieces for them. Older children, those 4 years and up, can cut out and create the craft themselves.

MATERIALS LIST

Each child needs:
◇ A pencil
◇ Scissors
◇ Glue
◇ Blue, yellow, red, orange, and black construction paper
◇ A dark crayon
◇ A paper punch
◇ Cartoons from the Sunday newspaper

DIRECTIONS

Instruct the children as follows: "Use the pattern to trace 16 colorful cartoon feathers. The easiest way is to fold the newspaper into a thickness of eight sheets. Trace 2 feathers on the top sheet. Cut out 8 feathers at a time.

"Use the patterns to trace a body onto yellow construction paper, a beak and two feet onto orange paper, and a wattle onto red paper. Cut out the pieces. Make two black eyes using the paper punch and black paper.

"Lay the turkey body on a sheet of blue construction paper. Stick the flat end of the cartoon feathers under the body and arrange them in a fan shape. Then glue them in place.

"Glue on the two feet. Fold the beak in half (as shown on the pattern). Glue it on the turkey's face. Add the red wattle and the paper-punch eyes. Hang your picture up to decorate for Thanksgiving."

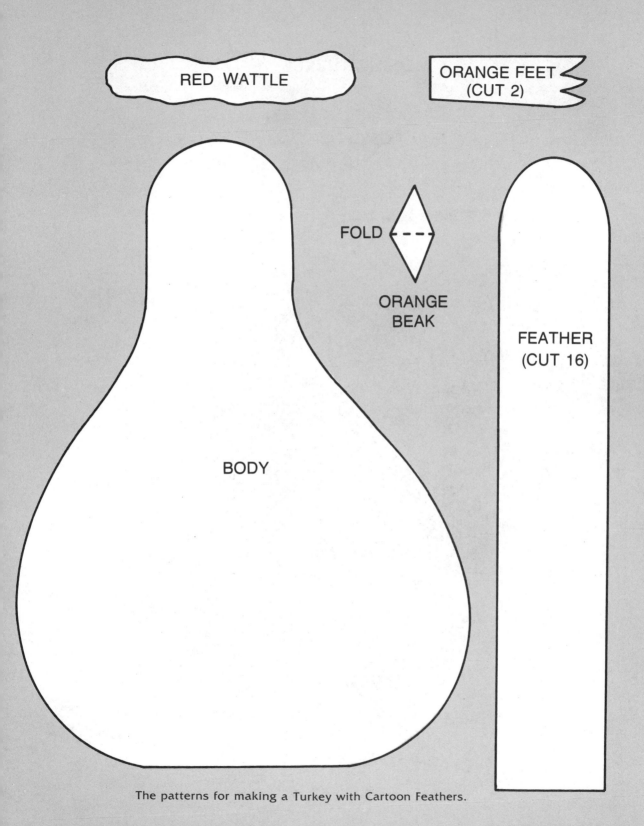

RED WATTLE

ORANGE FEET
(CUT 2)

FOLD - - - -

ORANGE
BEAK

BODY

FEATHER
(CUT 16)

The patterns for making a Turkey with Cartoon Feathers.

MOSAIC TURKEY

This turkey makes a perfect picture for November. The finished mosaic is slipped into a plastic bag, which keeps loose seeds from falling on the floor.

AGE GROUP

Mosaic Turkey is simple, and yet complex enough to interest all children from ages 2 to 10.

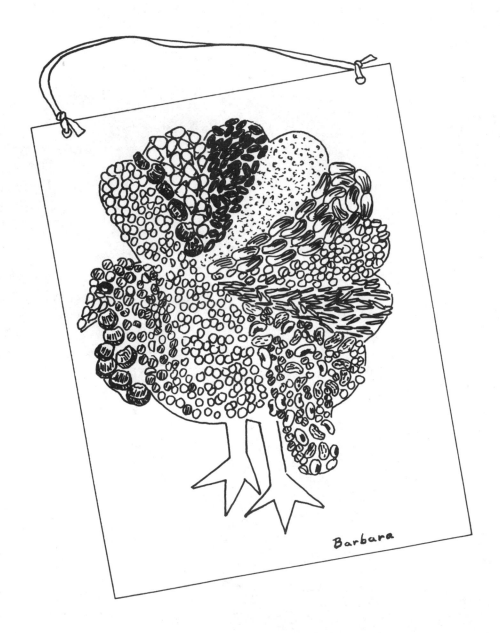

MATERIALS LIST

Each child needs:
◇ Newspaper
◇ 2 sheets of construction paper 9″ × 12″
◇ A black marker
◇ Scissors
◇ Glue
◇ 5 or more different kinds of seeds, such as:
   Unpopped popcorn, Dried split peas, Dried beans,
   Rice, Grass seed, Bird seed, Sesame seed
◇ A plastic food storage bag 11″ × 13″
◇ A paper punch
◇ Ribbon or yarn

DIRECTIONS

Pour each type of seed into a separate bowl. Then tell the children the following:

"Cover your work surface with newspapers to catch stray seeds. Use the pattern to trace the turkey onto construction paper. Draw lines on the turkey for feathers (as shown on the pattern). Cut out the turkey. Glue it onto a sheet of construction paper.

"Spread glue on one part of the turkey, such as on one feather. Pour one type of seed onto the glued area. Some of the seeds will stick to the glue. Turn the picture on end, dumping the excess seed back into its bowl.

"Spread glue on another part of the turkey. Pour on another type of seed; then pour off the excess as before. Repeat this process until all or most of the turkey is covered in seeds of different colors and textures.

"When you are finished, slip the Mosaic Turkey into the plastic bag. Punch two holes through both paper and plastic at the top of the picture. Tie a piece of ribbon or yarn through the holes to hang it up."

IMPORTANT: Let Mosaic Turkey dry flat overnight or the seeds might slide off. If the picture bends, tape a piece of cardboard 2 × 9 inches on the back just below the holes.

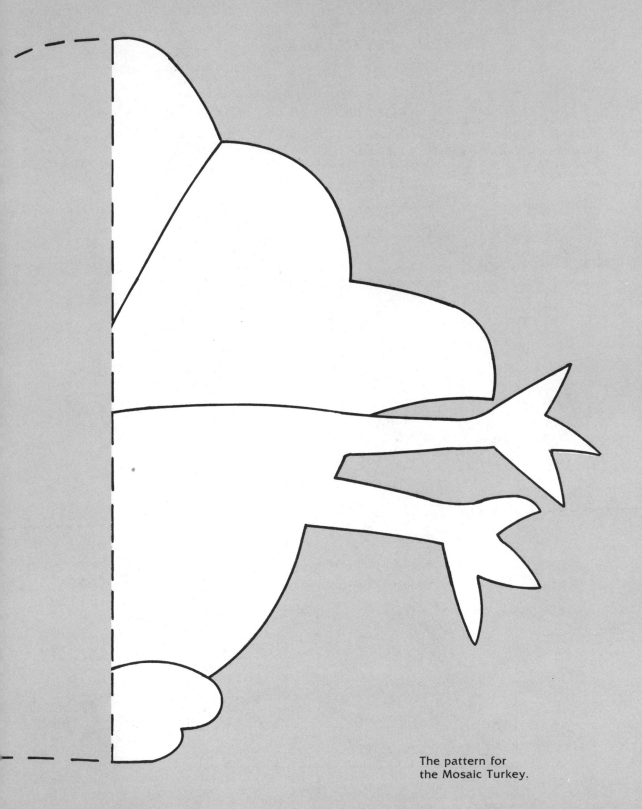

The pattern for
the Mosaic Turkey.

Mosaic Turkey   195

SHAPES CANDLE

Pilgrims made candles from *tallow*, the hard fat of animals. They used the candles to light their simple homes.

AGE GROUP

Shapes Candle is a four-piece puzzle for preschoolers as young as 2. As they glue the candle pieces, they can learn the names of the rectangle, square, diamond, and triangle.

MATERIALS LIST

Each child needs:
◇ A ruler
◇ A pencil
◇ Scissors
◇ Glue
◇ Red, yellow, orange, green, and blue construction paper

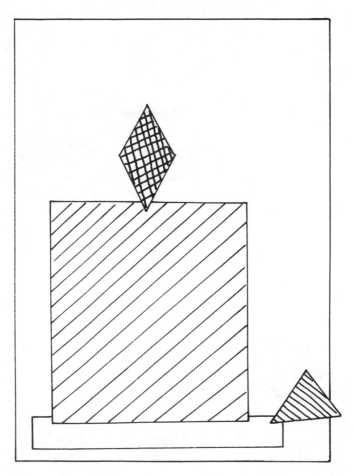

DIRECTIONS

Tell the children: "Use the pencil and ruler to draw a square 5 × 5 inches on red construction paper. Draw a yellow rectangle 2 × 7 inches.

"Use the patterns to draw an orange diamond and a green triangle. Cut out the four shapes." You can do these steps for younger children, but encourage children 4 years old and up to try it themselves.

Each child can arrange the shapes to form a candle. Then he can glue them on a sheet of blue paper. As he handles the shapes, help him learn their names by saying, "That shape is a *red square* (or *yellow rectangle*, or *orange diamond*)." Then ask, "What shape is it? That's right. It's a *red square*." He can also count the shapes with you as he glues them.

"Use the paper punch to make four or five holes in each end of the canoe (as shown on the pattern). Tie a piece of yarn through the first hole. Wrap a piece of tape around the end of the yarn, forming a stiff "needle." Use this needle to sew down through the holes and then sew back up. Tie the two ends of yarn together in a knot. Sew the other side of the canoe the same way.

"Use the pattern to draw two seats on cardboard. Cut them out. Fold down both ends. Staple the seats inside the canoe to hold it open."

The children can make clothespin dolls to occupy their Indian village. *Crafts for Kids: A Month-By-Month Idea Book* shows you how. They can use brown cloth and black yarn to make the dolls look like Indians.

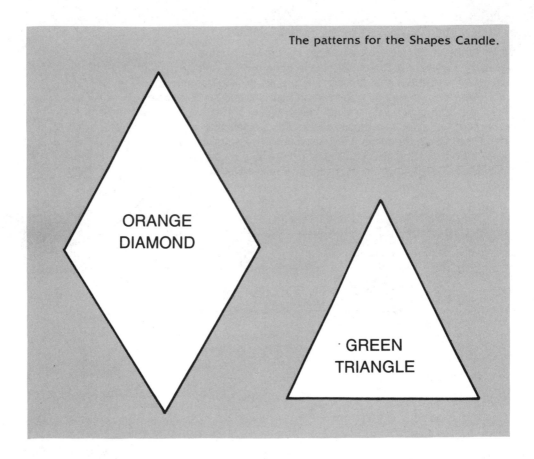

The patterns for the Shapes Candle.

ORANGE DIAMOND

GREEN TRIANGLE

TEPEE AND CANOE

American Indians made a tepee to live in by draping animal skins around poles. They made a canoe of birch bark to glide noiselessly on the lakes and rivers.

AGE GROUP

Children from ages 2 to 7 can learn about the Indians of the past by making a paper tepee and canoe. They can draw pretend Indian signs on them, too. Older children can create a whole Indian village.

MATERIALS LIST

Each child needs:
◇ Water-based markers
◇ Brown construction paper or a grocery bag
◇ Scissors
◇ Glue
◇ A paper punch
◇ Yarn
◇ A stapler
◇ Cardboard

DIRECTIONS

Instruct the children as follows: "Fold the brown construction paper (or grocery bag paper) in half. Place the bottom of the canoe pattern on the fold. Cut out the canoe through both thicknesses of paper.

"Use the tepee pattern to trace and cut out a tepee. Decorate the tepee and canoe with pretend Indian signs.

"Curl the tepee into a cone shape with a small hole at the top. Glue the side to make it hold its shape. The hole lets out smoke from the Indian's cooking and heating fire. Cut a slit in the tepee (as shown on the pattern). Fold it back to make a door.

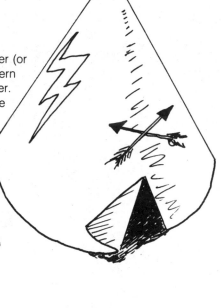

The pattern for making the canoe.

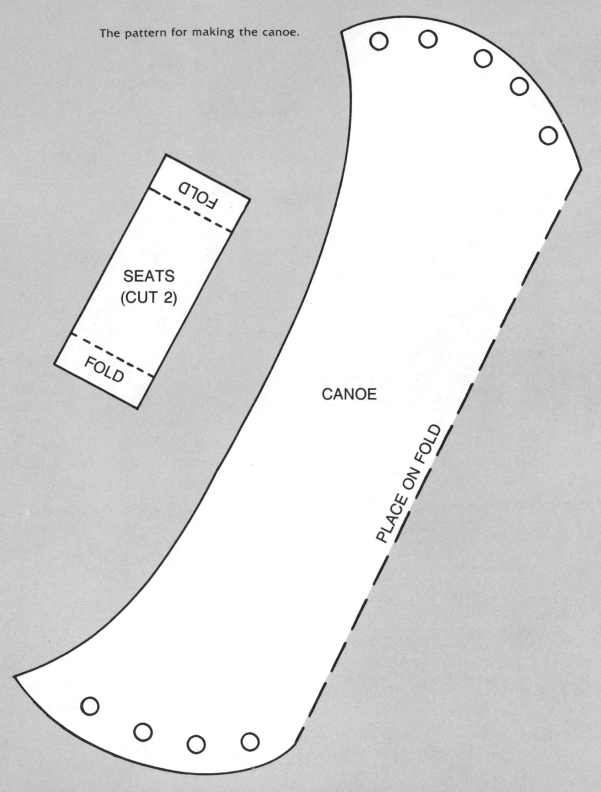

SEATS
(CUT 2)

FOLD

FOLD

CANOE

PLACE ON FOLD

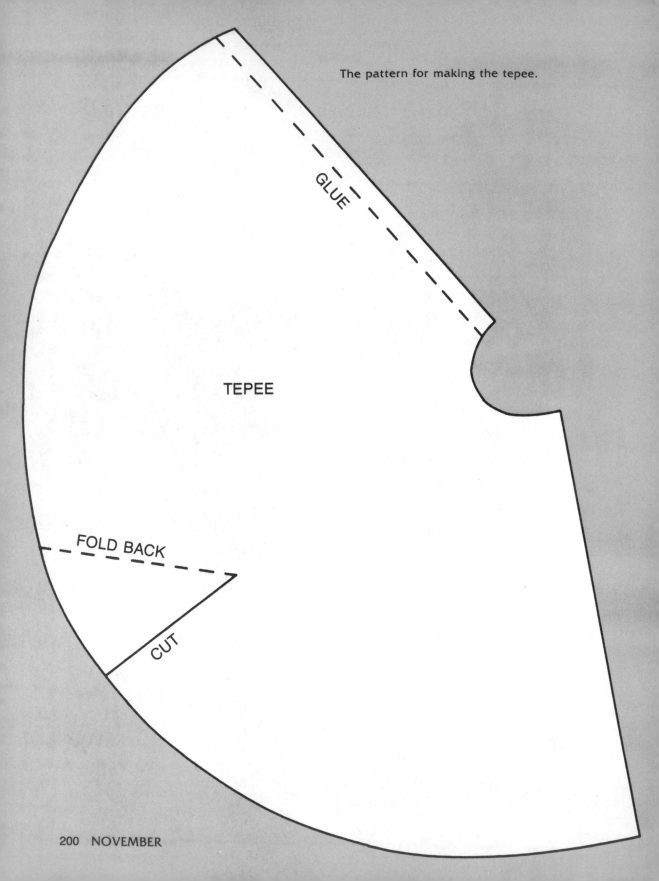

The pattern for making the tepee.

GLUE

TEPEE

FOLD BACK

CUT

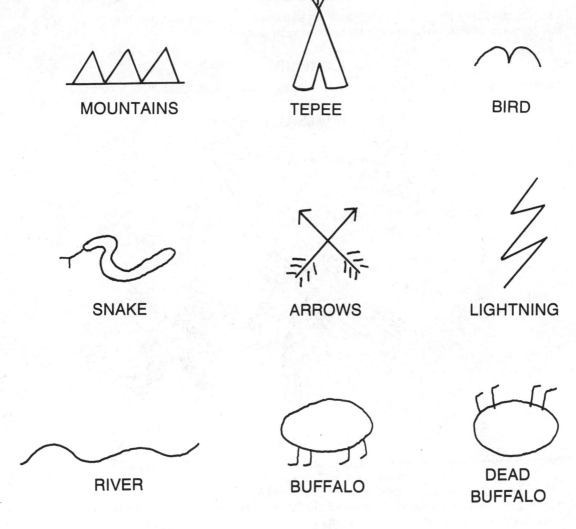

MOUNTAINS

TEPEE

BIRD

SNAKE

ARROWS

LIGHTNING

RIVER

BUFFALO

DEAD
BUFFALO

Pretend Indian Signs.

YARN DOLLS

A Pilgrim child's first doll was made by hand, just as these old-fashioned yarn dolls are. They can be made of yarn, embroidery floss, or long, fresh grass.

AGE GROUP

Children 6 years old and up can make these dolls for themselves or for younger friends.

MATERIALS LIST

Each child needs:
◇ 2 skeins of embroidery floss in different colors
◇ Scissors

DIRECTIONS

Tell the children: "Wrap one-half skein of embroidery floss around three fingers (about 3 inches). Tie it near the top to make the head and neck.

"Wrap one-half skein of a different color of embroidery floss around two fingers (about 2 inches). Put this floss through the center of the doll, just below the neck to form the doll's arms. Tie below the arms to make the waist.

"Tie wrists on both ends of the arms. Then cut the ends to make hands.

"To make a girl doll, cut the end of the floss at the bottom of the doll. Flare the ends out to make a skirt.

"To make a boy doll, divide the floss at the bottom of the doll into two pieces. Tie them to make ankles. Then cut the ends of the floss to make feet."

HOLIDAY NAPKIN RINGS

Made of toilet-paper rolls, Holiday Napkin Rings will brighten a supper table. The children can cover them with fall wrapping paper for Thanksgiving, with birthday paper for a party, or with Christmas paper or Hanukkah wrap for December festivities.

AGE GROUP

This craft is suitable for all ages. The children should make enough napkin rings for everyone who will be at the holiday table.

MATERIALS LIST

Each child needs:
◇ A ruler
◇ A pencil
◇ Scissors
◇ Glue
◇ Wrapping paper
◇ Toilet-paper rolls

DIRECTIONS

Instruct the children as follows: "Use the pencil and ruler to measure 3- x -6-inch rectangles on the wrapping paper. Measure and cut out one rectangle for each napkin ring.

"Cut each toilet-paper roll into sections 1 ½ inches long. Do this by squeezing the roll flat, cutting straight across it, then opening the cut sections into a circle again. The wrapping paper will cover the crease and add stiffness to the rings.

"Spread glue on the back of the wrapping paper. Wrap the paper around the toilet-paper roll. Tuck the extra paper into the top and bottom of the roll. Press it down smoothly with your fingers. Repeat until you have made as many napkin rings as you need. Let them dry.

"To use the rings, pull the corner of a cloth or large paper supper napkin through the ring until the ring is holding the napkin in the middle.

"Lay the napkin to the left of the fork at the table, or put it in the center of the supper plate. People will sit down at the table and remove the napkin from the Holiday Napkin Ring to use it."

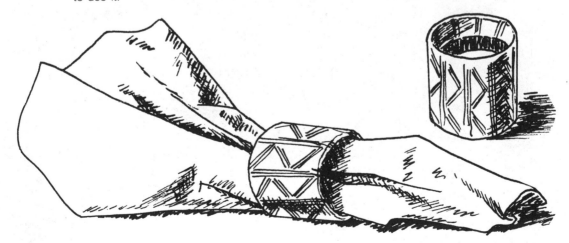

HANDY ART

Trace around a child's hand to create different pictures. Use the ideas here, and maybe your child can think of new ones.

AGE GROUP

Children 2 years old and up can use their imaginations with this craft.

MATERIALS LIST

Each child needs:
◇ Paper
◇ A pencil
◇ Crayons or markers
◇ Scissors (optional)

DIRECTIONS

Use your child's hand as a pattern. He should lay his hand, palm down, on a sheet of paper. Trace around his hand with a pencil. He can color the traced shape to turn it into different pictures. He can cut it out and mount it on construction paper if he wants.

HAND PRINT INDIAN

MAKE A FIST.
STICK UP TWO FINGERS
AND TRACE AROUND.

HANDY ART BUNNY

HANDY ART GOOSE

HANDY ART TREE

WHOLE HAND GHOST

HAND PRINT TURKEY

PUMPKIN COOKIES

Move over, pumpkin pie! These soft, moist cookies are so good with a glass of cold milk that the children won't even realize how nutritious they are.

MATERIALS NEEDED

◇ A large bowl
◇ A wooden spoon
◇ A cookie sheet or two
◇ Solid shortening for greasing the cookie sheet
◇ 1 cup brown sugar, firmly packed
◇ 1 cup pumpkin
◇ ½ cup oil
◇ 1 egg
◇ 1 teaspoon vanilla
◇ 2½ cups flour (Use whole wheat or all-purpose flour.)
◇ 1 teaspoon soda
◇ 1 teaspoon baking powder
◇ ½ teaspoon salt
◇ ½ teaspoon cinnamon
◇ ½ teaspoon nutmeg
◇ ¼ teaspoon ginger
◇ 1 cup raisins (optional)
◇ ½ cup chopped nuts (optional)

DIRECTIONS

Show the children how to grease the cookie sheet, using their fingers and solid shortening. After they wash their hands, give them a large bowl and a wooden spoon.

Help them measure the brown sugar, pumpkin, oil, egg, and vanilla into the bowl. The children should stir until these ingredients are thoroughly mixed.

Then they should add the flour, soda, baking powder, salt, cinnamon, nutmeg, and ginger. Let them stir until the dough is smooth. Add the nuts and raisins if your children like them. Mine don't.

Help the children drop the dough from a teaspoon onto the greased cookie sheet. Place the cookies a little apart.

Bake in a preheated oven at 350° F for 12 minutes, until the cookies are dry on top. Do not overbake. This recipe makes about three dozen cookies, depending on how much dough is eaten before the cookies are baked.

DECEMBER
CRAFTS

December is my favorite time of year with the wonderful celebrations of Christmas and Hanukkah to brighten the dark days. Each year around December 20, our family hosts a Children's Gingerbread Boy Party. The day before the party we bake dozens of gingerbread boys and string a ribbon through the top of each one. On the day of the party, we make a double batch of buttercream frosting, tint it with food color, and divide it into several small pastry bags. We place little bowls on the kitchen table, filled with all kinds of decorations, including: colored sugar, coconut, raisins, gumdrops, chocolate chips, M&Ms, nuts, and decorating candies found in the grocery store.

Our guests soon learn to work the pastry bags, and they decorate several gingerbread boys each while their parents visit over refreshments.

As each cookie is finished, it's slipped into a plastic sandwich bag for the trip home. There it can be hung on the tree to be admired, and then eaten for breakfast Christmas morning.

The 11 crafts in this chapter will give the children plenty to do while they wait for the holidays. The Cylinder and Cone Tree, for instance, gives them hands-on experience with geometric shapes, and the finished tree gives them a feeling of accomplishment. The third grade made this tree. They're tired of writing letters now, but they did come up with these.

Dear Mrs. Dondiego,
    Thank you for making the tree with us. The cilender was hard but I think I will live.
                                                        Love, Laura

Dear Mrs. Dondiego,
    Thank you for comming in and helping our class make the Christmas tree. I don't no what I'm going to do with the Christmas tree. But I'm shur that I can think of something.
                                                        Love, Lynn

CYLINDER AND CONE TREE

Children get hands-on experience with geometric shapes while creating this beautiful Christmas decoration.

AGE GROUP

This tree is easier than it looks. With adult help, even preschoolers can make one. It's a favorite with children through age 10.

MATERIALS LIST

Each child needs:
◇ A pencil
◇ A ruler
◇ Green, yellow, and white construction paper
◇ Scissors
◇ Glue
◇ A pipe cleaner (Look in the Tobacco section of drugstores.)
◇ A few cotton balls
◇ Crimped paper ribbon, cut 22 inches long
◇ Glitter (Look in the School Supplies section of drugstores.)

DIRECTIONS

Instruct the children as follows: "Using a pencil and ruler, measure and draw a 3½- x -10-inch rectangle onto green construction paper. Cut it out and roll it to form a 10-inch cylinder. Overlap the edges ½ inch and glue the cylinder to make it hold its shape."

You will need to help children under the age of 5 or 6, but let older children try this themselves. Then tell them:

"This is the tree trunk. Set it aside to dry.

"Use the pattern to trace the cone shape onto green construction paper. Cut it out. To form the cone, hold the cone shape with the flat edge at the top. Holding it at each point, pull your two hands together and downward. Overlap the edges until the paper comes to a sharp point at the top. Glue the cone to make it hold its shape. Set it aside to dry.

"Use the pattern to trace the circle base onto white construction paper. Carefully cut out the small circle in the middle. Now the tree is ready to be put together.

"Draw four lines, each 2 inches long, down both ends of the cylinder. Make sure the lines are spaced evenly apart. Cut on the lines to form four tabs at each end of the cylinder. Bend these tabs out.

"Apply glue to the inside of the four tabs on one end of the cylinder. Insert this end of the cylinder into the green cone. Gently press the glued tabs with your fingers so they will stick to the inside walls of the cone. Make sure the cylinder is in straight, or your tree will be crooked when it's finished.

"Now apply glue to the outside of the four tabs on the other end of the cylinder. Insert this end through the center hole of the white circle base. Gently press the glued tabs against the bottom of the base. If the tree does not want to stand by itself, stuff the trunk from the bottom with a few extra cotton balls. Then glue a 2-inch square of cardboard to the bottom of the circle base to add weight and stability.

"Fold a small piece of yellow construction paper in half. Use the pattern to draw a star, with the top of the pattern placed on the folded edge. When you cut the star out (do not cut through the folded edge) you will have two stars fastened together at the top.

"Apply glue between the stars, and insert one end of the pipe cleaner between them. Carefully press the stars together.

"Put a dab of glue on one end of the paper ribbon. Insert this end in the very top of the tree, along with the pipe cleaner that holds the star. Wrap the rest of the ribbon loosely around the tree. Put a dab of glue on the other end of the ribbon and anchor it onto the bottom of the cone.

"Spread glue on the circle base, and stick on bits of cotton to look like snow. Add a few dots of glue to the cone. Sift on glitter."

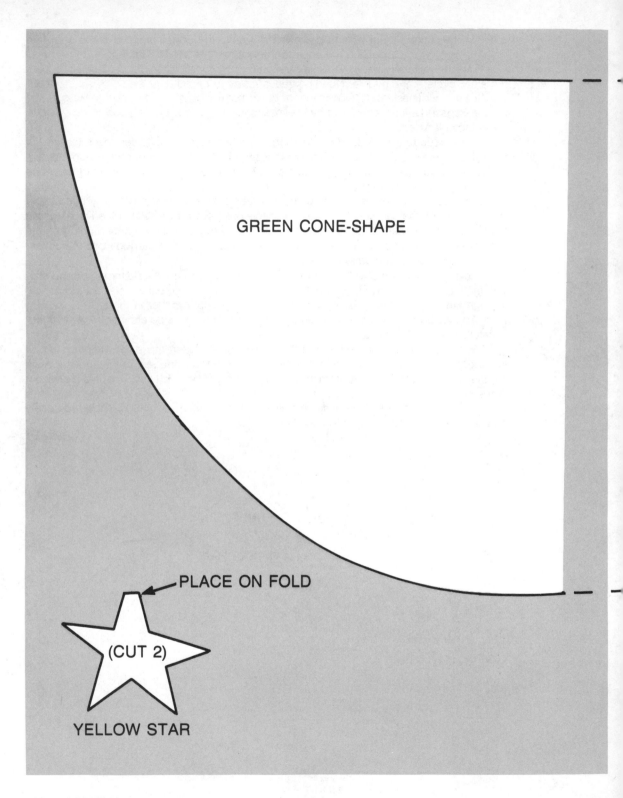

GREEN CONE-SHAPE

PLACE ON FOLD

(CUT 2)

YELLOW STAR

WHITE CIRCLE BASE

CUT OUT

The pattern for Cylinder and Cone Tree's base.

CHRISTMAS CANDLE

The Christmas Candle stands by itself to make a lovely table decoration.

AGE GROUP

This craft was designed for children from ages 8 to 10. Younger children can make the Christmas Candle with a lot of adult help.

MATERIALS LIST

Each child needs:
◇ A pencil
◇ A ruler
◇ Scissors
◇ Glue
◇ White, yellow, and red construction paper
◇ 4 cotton balls
◇ Glitter

DIRECTIONS

Tell the children the following: "Use the pencil and ruler to draw a rectangle 5½ × 10 inches onto white construction paper. Roll the rectangle into a cylinder 10 inches long to make the candle. Overlap the edge of the cylinder 1½ inches and glue it to hold its shape.

"Use the pencil and ruler to draw four 2-inch lines down one end of the cylinder. Space them equally apart. Cut on these lines. Fold out the cut ends to make four tabs. Set the candle aside while you make the circle base.

"Use the pattern to trace the circle base onto yellow construction paper. Cut out and discard the smaller circle in the center.

"Slide the circle over the top of the candle. Put glue on the upper side of the four tabs. Press the tabs against the bottom of the circle base. Now the candle will stand by itself.

"To make the flame, fold yellow construction paper in half. Place the top of the large flame pattern on the fold. Trace onto the paper. Cut out the piece to make two large yellow flames fastened together at the top.

"Apply glue to the outside of the flames' long ends. Insert the ends in the top of the candle. Press the glued ends against the insides of the candle to make them stay in place.

"Use the small flame pattern to trace two flames onto red paper. Cut out. Glue a red flame in the center of each yellow flame.

"Spread glue on the circle base. Pull the cotton balls apart and stick cotton to the base to look like snow.

"Spread glue on the red flames and in loops around the top of the candle to look like melted wax. Sift glitter onto the glue."

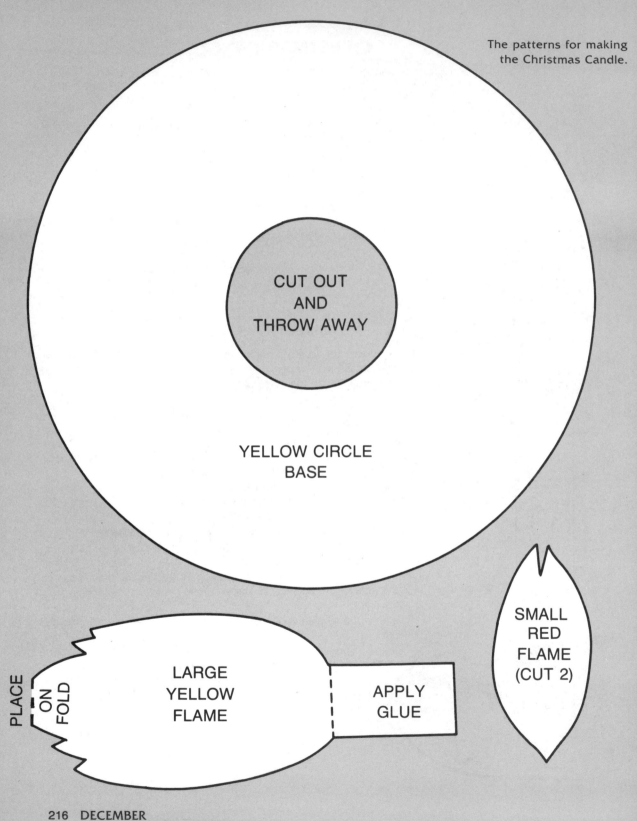

The patterns for making the Christmas Candle.

CUT OUT
AND
THROW AWAY

YELLOW CIRCLE
BASE

SMALL
RED
FLAME
(CUT 2)

PLACE

ON
FOLD

LARGE
YELLOW
FLAME

APPLY
GLUE

STYROFOAM CUP BELL

Children love the magic created by glitter and sequins, especially at Christmas time. Jingle bells and sequins can be found in a variety store, craft shop, or fabric store.

AGE GROUP

This craft is easy enough for a 2-year-old to make with adult help, and elegant enough to interest a 10-year-old. Older children can make several bells and hang them in clusters of three or four.

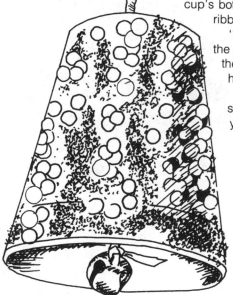

MATERIALS LIST

Each child needs:
◇ A plain white Styrofoam cup
◇ A yarn needle (Look in the Sewing Notions section of grocery and drug stores.)
◇ A narrow ribbon 18″ long
◇ A jingle bell
◇ Glue
◇ Sequins
◇ Glitter

DIRECTIONS

Instruct the children as follows: "Thread the yarn needle with the ribbon. On one end of the ribbon, tie the jingle bell with a knot.

"Put the needle inside the cup and punch it through the middle of the cup's bottom. Pull the needle through the cup and remove it from the ribbon. The jingle bell will be inside the cup.

"Tie a knot in the ribbon inside the cup, about 3 inches above the jingle bell. The knot will keep the bell in place. Tie a loop in the other end of the ribbon so the Styrofoam Cup Bell can be hung up when finished.

"Spread glue on part of the outside of the cup. Pour on the sequins. Continue spreading glue and pouring on sequins until you have as many sequins on as you want.

"Next pour glitter on the cup, adding more glue if it's needed. Return extra sequins and glitter to their containers. Hang your craft up to dry."

BELL MOBILE

This craft is simple but elegant, just right for holiday decorating.

AGE GROUP

The Bell Mobile was designed especially for children ages 2 to 8.

MATERIALS LIST

Each child needs:
◇ A pencil
◇ Scissors
◇ Glue
◇ Construction paper in light colors
◇ Crayons or markers
◇ A 24″ piece of crimped paper ribbon
◇ Glitter

DIRECTIONS

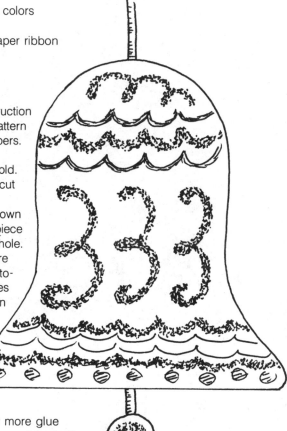

Instruct the children as follows: "Fold a piece of construction paper in half crosswise. Place the bottom of the bell pattern on the fold. Trace around it. Cut out through both papers. Do not cut the folded edge.

"Place the bottom of the clapper pattern on the fold. Trace around it. Cut out through both papers. Don't cut the folded edge.

"Cut a small hole in the bottom of the bell (as shown on the pattern). Open the bell and insert the 24-inch piece of ribbon down the length of the bell and through the hole.

"Pull the ribbon through the hole so 2 inches are hanging below the bell. Glue the halves of the bell together with the ribbon centered inside. Glue the halves of the clapper together below the bell, with the ribbon centered inside.

"Color the Bell Mobile on both sides with crayons and markers. Tie a loop in the top of the ribbon for hanging.

"Spread glue on one side of the mobile. Sprinkle on glitter. Dump the excess glitter onto a piece of paper and return it to its container.

"Hang up the mobile. When the glue is dry, apply more glue and glitter to the other side. Hang it up and let it dry several hours."

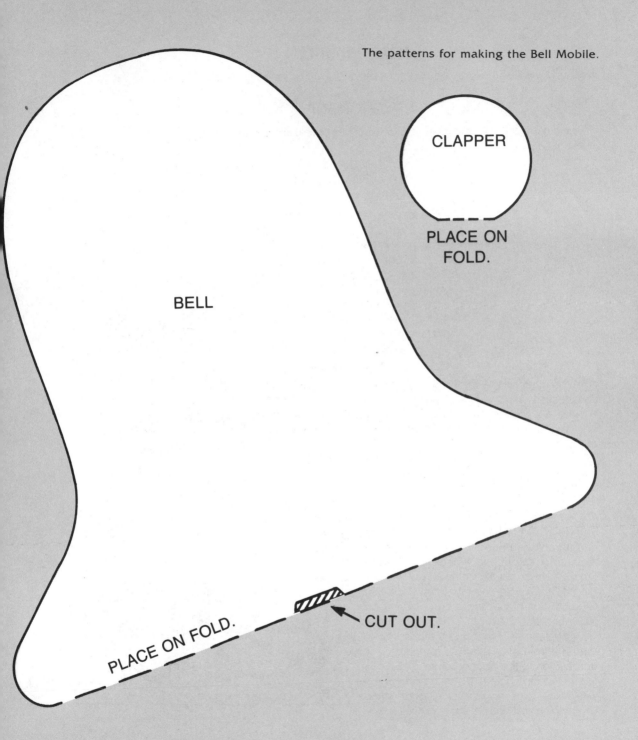

The patterns for making the Bell Mobile.

CLAPPER

PLACE ON
FOLD.

BELL

PLACE ON FOLD.

CUT OUT.

TREE MOBILE

Big and beautiful, the Tree Mobile hangs decoratively in a window, on a wall, or on a mirror.

AGE GROUP

This is a good craft for children ages 6 to 10 as they practice measuring and construction skills.

MATERIALS LIST

Each child needs:
◇ 2 sheets of green construction paper
◇ Brown construction paper
◇ A pencil
◇ A ruler
◇ Scissors
◇ Glue
◇ 36″ narrow crimped paper ribbon
◇ Glitter, stickers, rickrack, stick-on stars, any other bright decorations

DIRECTIONS

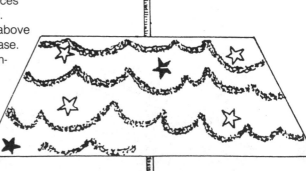

Give the children the following instructions: ''On a sheet of green construction paper, draw a triangle that is 12 inches tall and has a base 8¾ inches wide. Lay your drawing on a second sheet of green paper. Cut out the triangle through both thicknesses of paper.

"You should have two triangles. Measure the triangle into three pieces, each of them 4 inches tall. Once again, cut through both triangles together.

"Measure and cut out two brown rectangles 1½ x 2 inches. These will form the tree trunk. Spread glue between the tree trunk pieces. Lay one end of the ribbon in the center. Glue the pieces together so the ribbon is centered between them.

"Leave about 12 inches of ribbon exposed above the tree trunk. Spread glue on the widest tree base. Glue the two pieces together so the ribbon is centered between them.

"Repeat this process with the middle of the tree and the top of the tree, spreading on glue and centering the ribbon between them.

"Decorate both sides of the Tree Mobile with glitter, stickers, rickrack, stick-on stars, or anything else bright and beautiful.''

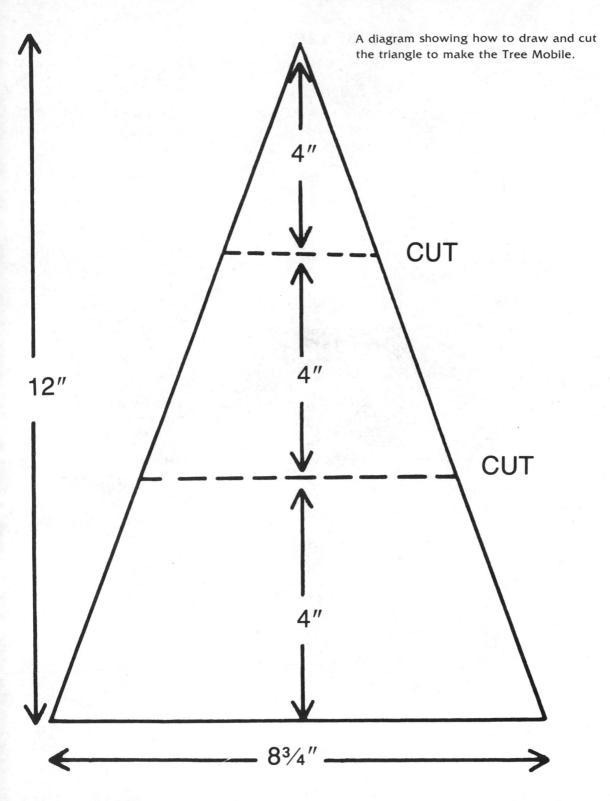

A diagram showing how to draw and cut the triangle to make the Tree Mobile.

4"

CUT

4"

CUT

4"

12"

8¾"

STAND-UP TREE

A few wisps of cotton give a wintry look to this table decoration.

AGE GROUP

If an adult does the tracing and cutting, this tree can be made by children as young as 2. It's a good craft for all children through age 10. Encourage children 4 years old and up to do their own tracing and cutting.

MATERIALS LIST

Each child needs:
◇ A pencil
◇ Scissors
◇ Glue
◇ Green and yellow construction paper
◇ A few cotton balls

DIRECTIONS

Instruct the children as follows: "Fold two sheets of green construction paper in half. Use the pattern to trace the tree shape onto both sheets of paper. Make sure that the flat side of the pattern is laying along the fold of the construction paper. Cut the pieces out through the double thickness of paper. When the cutouts are unfolded, you will have two whole trees.

"Trace the star onto yellow construction paper. Cut it out.

"Apply glue to half of each tree (as indicated on the pattern). Press the glued sides together so they match. Before the glue dries, pull the two sides apart at the top and insert the stem of the star. Press the two sides together again, with the star stem in place between them.

"Put a little bit of glue along the tree branches. Add a few very light wisps of cotton."

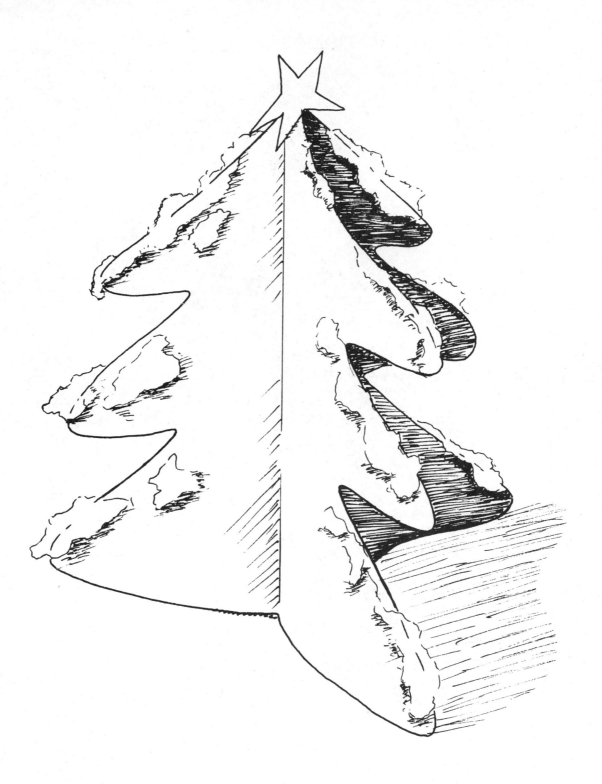

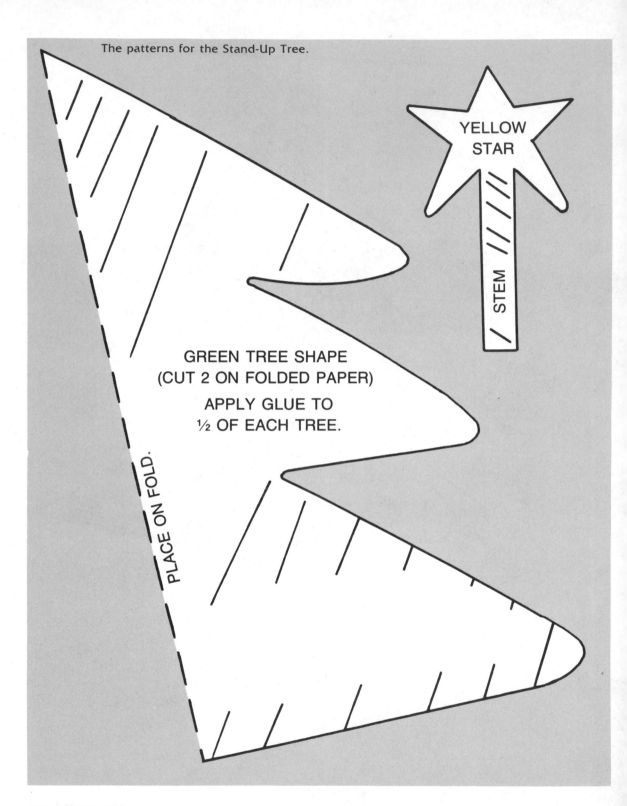

The patterns for the Stand-Up Tree.

YELLOW
STAR

STEM

GREEN TREE SHAPE
(CUT 2 ON FOLDED PAPER)

APPLY GLUE TO
½ OF EACH TREE.

PLACE ON FOLD.

CHRISTMAS ELF

Curls and more curls make the beard of this bright holiday decoration.

AGE GROUP

Children from ages 2 to 10 will enjoy making the Christmas Elf. Help the younger ones with tracing and cutting. Count the 10 curls with your preschoolers.

MATERIALS LIST

Each child needs:
◇ A 9″ white paper plate
◇ Red, white, and blue construction paper
◇ Scissors
◇ Glue
◇ A pencil
◇ A ruler
◇ A black marker
◇ A few cotton balls

DIRECTIONS

Instruct the children as follows: "Use the pattern to trace a red hat, red nose, red mouth, and two blue eyes onto construction paper. Cut out these pieces.

"Glue the hat onto the paper plate. Add the eyes, nose, and mouth. Draw eyeballs on the eyes with the black marker.

"Pull the cotton balls apart and glue pieces of cotton to the hat. Glue on cotton eyebrows and a cotton mustache.

"Cut a sheet of white construction paper into 10 strips, 1 x 9 inches each. Lay a strip on the table and roll up a pencil in it. Remove the pencil and the paper will remain curled. Repeat with the other strips. Glue the 10 curls around the edge of the elf's face to make a beard."

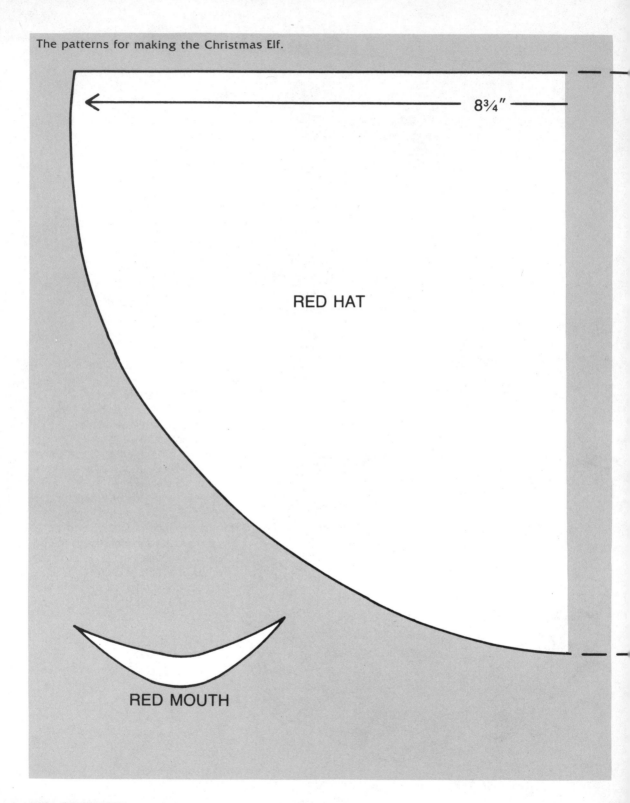

The patterns for making the Christmas Elf.

8¾"

RED HAT

RED MOUTH

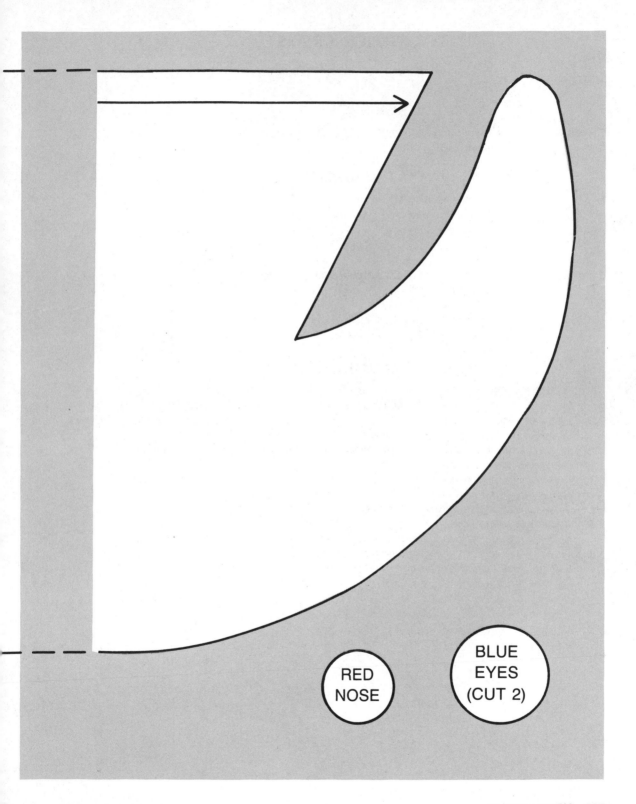

RED
NOSE

BLUE
EYES
(CUT 2)

TOOTHPICK CROSS

This is a lovely decoration for Christmas or Easter. We tape ours in the middle of the hallway mirror.

AGE GROUP

It takes a lot of dexterity and patience to glue 152 toothpicks to a cardboard base. Children 8 years old and up will enjoy this craft.

MATERIALS LIST

Each child needs:
◇ Newspapers to cover the work surface
◇ A pencil
◇ Scissors
◇ Glue
◇ Cardboard (Buy poster board, or cut up an old box.)
◇ 152 round toothpicks
◇ White glue
◇ Glitter (Look in the School Supplies section of grocery and drug stores.)

DIRECTIONS

Give the children the following directions: "Use the pattern to draw a cross on cardboard. Glue on four toothpicks in the shape of the cross by spreading glue on the cardboard and laying the toothpicks on it.

"Spread a heavy coating of glue below one of the horizontal toothpicks. Starting at the point where the four toothpicks meet, glue twelve toothpicks side by side, with the point of each one touching the horizontal toothpick.

"Glue eight toothpicks horizontally on the arm of the cross, with their points touching the last toothpick from the previous step.

"Glue eight or nine toothpicks down one side of the vertical toothpick, with the point of each one touching it.

"Repeat this process with the rest of the cross. At the top and bottom of the cross, glue the toothpicks end to end, covering the cardboard completely.

"Lay the cross flat overnight to dry. Then spread glue on it with your finger, sprinkle with glitter, and let it dry again.

The pattern for the Toothpick Cross.

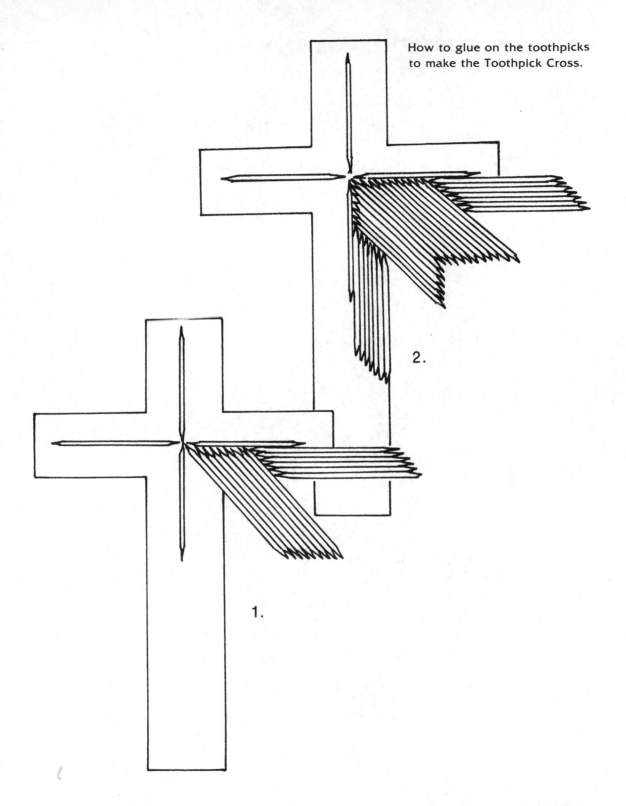

How to glue on the toothpicks
to make the Toothpick Cross.

2.

1.

TOOTHPICK STAR OF DAVID

This Hanukkah decoration can be set on a table or hung up with tape.

AGE GROUP

Children 8 years old and up will enjoy making the Star of David. It is made of 148 round toothpicks and two equilateral triangles.

MATERIALS LIST

Each child needs:
◇ White or blue poster board
◇ A ruler
◇ A pencil
◇ Scissors
◇ White glue
◇ 148 round toothpicks
◇ Brown shoe polish
◇ A soft rag (optional)
◇ Blue model paint
◇ A brush (optional)

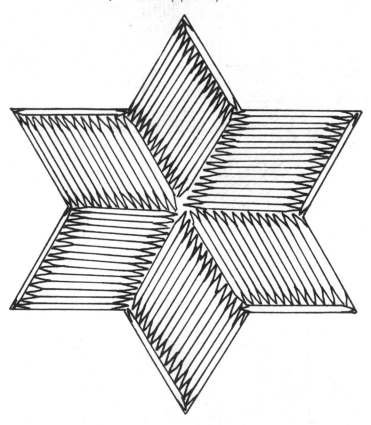

DIRECTIONS

Tell the children the following directions: "Use the ruler and pencil to draw two equilateral triangles (all sides equal) with 8-inch sides onto the poster board. Cut out the triangles. Turn one triangle upside down on top of the other to make a star shape. Glue in place so that the side of each star point is as long as one toothpick. In other words, use a toothpick as a measuring tool to make sure the triangles are in the right position before gluing them together.

"Outline the star with glue. Line up a single row of toothpicks around the edges. Spread glue on the star and line up toothpicks along one side of each star point.

"When the star is filled with toothpicks, lay a heavy book on it to keep it flat. Let it dry."

The star can be stained by rubbing with a little shoe polish on a soft cloth, or it can be painted blue with model paint.

1. How to glue on the toothpicks to make the Toothpick Star of David.

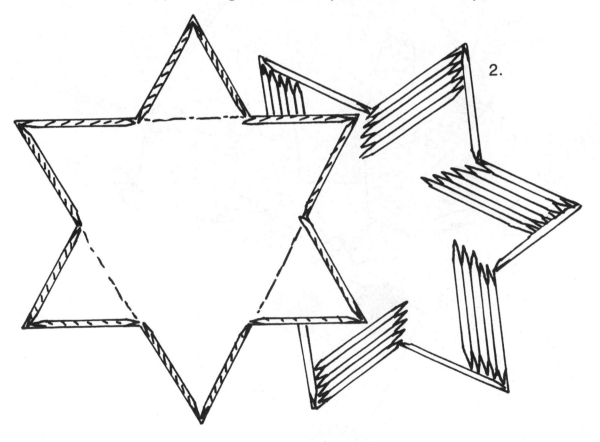

2.

REINDEER CARD HOLDER

Santa's reindeer (Rudolf, of course) hangs up anywhere to hold Christmas mail.

AGE GROUP

The Reindeer Card Holder is a useful craft for children ages 2 through 10. Preschoolers learn to create with a triangle and circles.

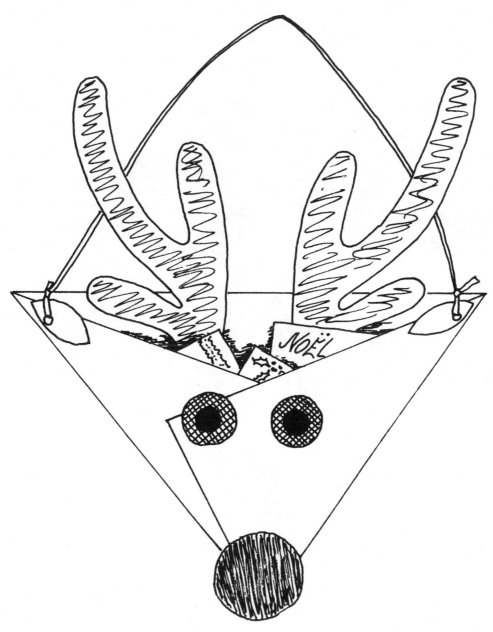

MATERIALS LIST

Each child needs:
◇ A pencil
◇ Scissors
◇ Glue
◇ A black marker
◇ Yellow, green, red, brown, and
  pink construction paper
◇ A paper punch
◇ 24″ narrow crimped paper ribbon

DIRECTIONS

Tell the children the following: "Fold a sheet of yellow construction paper to make a triangle. Glue one flap over the other to make a pocket.

"Use the patterns to trace two green antlers, two brown circle eyes, a red circle nose, and two pink ears onto construction paper.

"Glue the antlers on the triangle face. Add the eyes, nose, and ears. Draw eyeballs with a black marker.

"Make a hole in each ear with the paper punch. (The extra thickness of paper will help prevent the paper from ripping when ribbon is tied on.)

"Tie a 24-inch piece of ribbon in the holes so the reindeer can be hung up. Hang him on a doorknob, a wall, or a door. Fill him with holiday cards and letters."

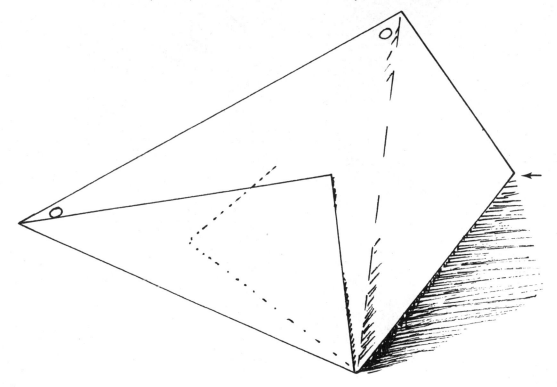

How to fold the paper to make the Reindeer Card Holder.

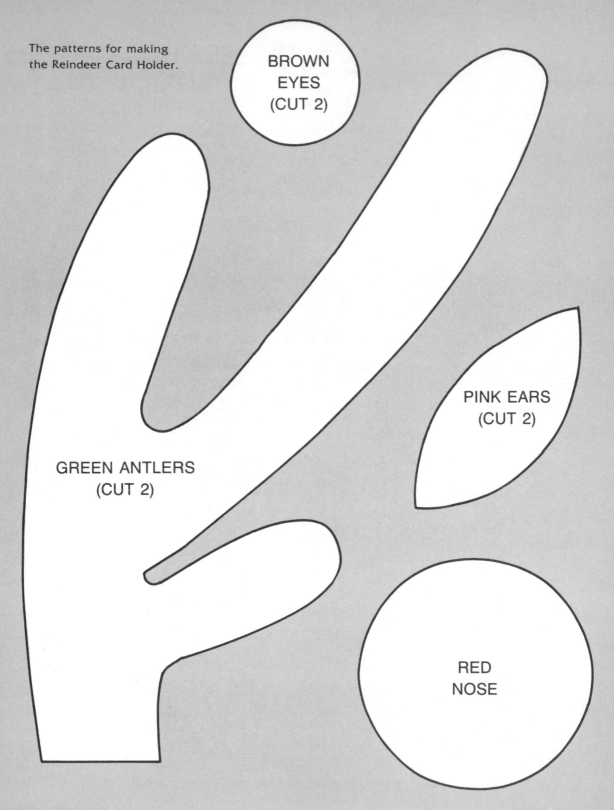

The patterns for making the Reindeer Card Holder.

BROWN EYES (CUT 2)

GREEN ANTLERS (CUT 2)

PINK EARS (CUT 2)

RED NOSE

ANGEL PENCIL HOLDER

Make this Angel from three circles and a rectangle. It can be given as a gift.

AGE GROUP

With adult help, this craft can be made by children from ages 2 to 7. Older children like to make their own creations from the orange-juice can.

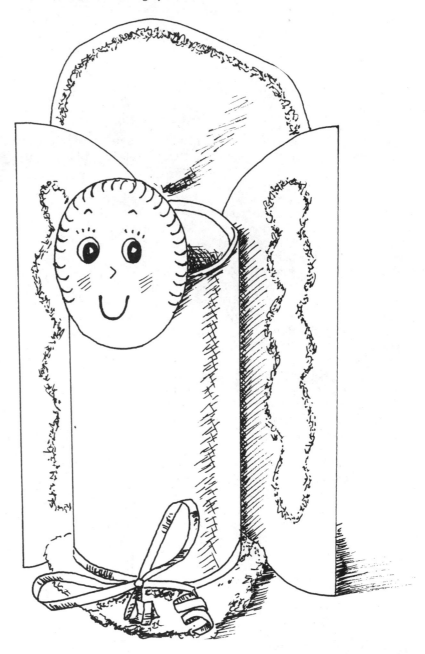

MATERIALS LIST

Each child needs:
◇ A pencil
◇ A ruler
◇ Scissors
◇ Glue in a squeeze bottle
◇ White and yellow construction paper
◇ A 12-oz. orange-juice can
◇ Several cotton balls
◇ White crimped paper ribbon
◇ Glitter
◇ Wax paper
◇ Markers and crayons

DIRECTIONS

Instruct the children as follows: "Measure and draw a rectangle 5 x 9 inches on white construction paper. Cut it out. Spread glue on it and wrap it around the orange-juice can, covering the can completely. This is the angel's body.

"Squeeze a thin line of glue around the bottom edge of the body. Cover the glue with pieces of cotton to make a cloud. Tie a piece of white crimped ribbon in a bow above the cotton.

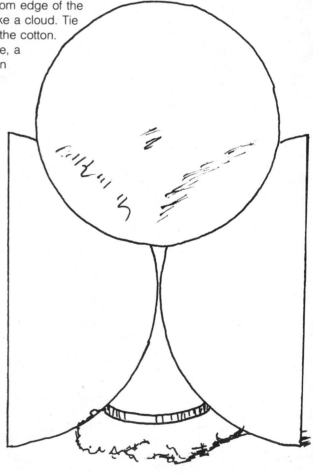

"Use the pattern to draw a large white circle, a medium yellow circle, and a small white circle on construction paper. Cut out the circles. Fold the large white circle in half. Cut on the fold. These two half circles are the angel's wings. Glue the wings to the back of the body so the rounded edges meet.

"The medium yellow circle is a halo. Glue it behind the wings, letting it stick up as much as possible.

"The small white circle is the angel's face. Use crayons and markers to color it, adding hair, eyes, nose, mouth, and rosy cheeks. Glue the face onto the front of the body, with half of it sticking up over the rim of the can.

"Squeeze a thin line of glue around the top of the halo. Add more glue to the wings.

"Hold the angel over wax paper and sift glitter onto the glue. Use the wax paper to return the excess glitter to its bottle.

"Make a card to put inside the pencil holder. It could say, *From Your Little Angel, (sign your name).* Give this craft to someone you love."

The patterns for the Angel Pencil Holder.

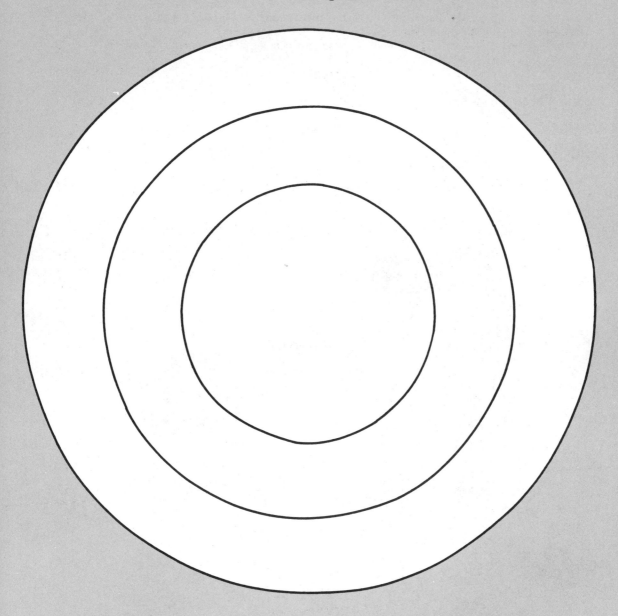

GINGERBREAD BOYS

Use a crochet hook to string ribbon, yarn, or embroidery thread through each baked cookie. Push the hook through the cookie, grab the ribbon, and pull it back through the hole. Decorate the cookie and hang it on the tree. Gingerbread and pine needles smell wonderful together!

AGE GROUP

With adult help, even the youngest child can decorate a gingerbread boy.

MATERIALS LIST

◇ ⅓ cup shortening
◇ 1 cup brown sugar, packed
◇ 1½ cups molasses
◇ ⅔ cup water
◇ 8 cups flour
◇ 2 teaspoons baking soda
◇ 1 teaspoon salt
◇ 1 teaspoon allspice
◇ 1 teaspoon cinnamon
◇ 1 teaspoon cloves
◇ 1 teaspoon ginger
◇ Greased baking sheets
◇ A rolling pin
◇ Gingerbread boy cookie cutter
◇ A crochet hook
◇ Ribbons
◇ Frosting and cookie decorations
(These follow.)

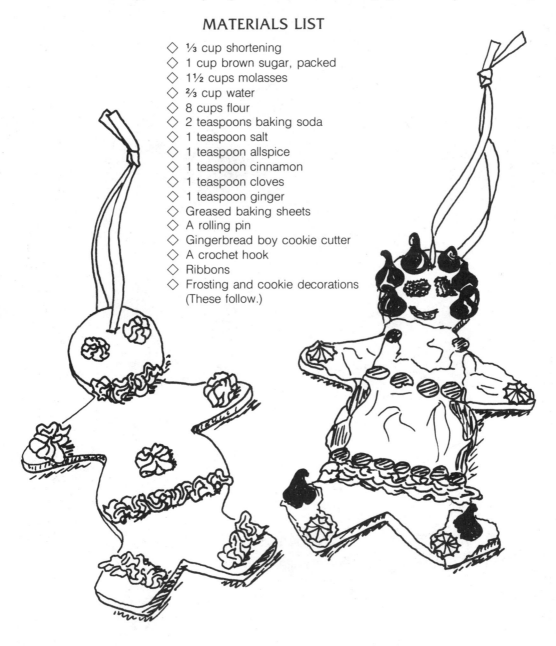

DIRECTIONS

To save time, an adult can do all the baking, and the children can do all the decorating of the baked cookies.

Mix together the shortening, brown sugar, and molasses. Stir in the water. Add the flour, baking soda, salt, allspice, cinnamon, cloves, and ginger. Mix the dough until all ingredients are thoroughly blended.

Cover the dough and refrigerate for 1 hour or longer. Roll out the dough on a floured surface. Roll out a small amount at a time, about ¼ inch thick.

Dip the gingerbread boy cutter in flour, cut out the dough, and transfer the gingerbread boys to a greased cookie sheet.

Bake at 350° F. for 10 to 12 minutes, until the cookies become firm and turn very light brown around the edges.

When the cookies have cooled, string a ribbon through each one, using the crochet hook. Frost with Buttercream Frosting.

BUTTERCREAM FROSTING

This recipe can be doubled. Cover and refrigerate leftovers.

MATERIALS LIST

◇ ½ cup shortening
◇ ½ cup margarine (1 stick)
◇ 1½ teaspoons vanilla
◇ 5½ cups sifted confectioners' sugar
◇ ¼ cup + 1 tablespoon milk
◇ Food coloring
◇ Decorations (colored sugar, coconut,
   raisins, gumdrops, chocolate chips, M&Ms, nuts)
◇ Several small pastry bags with decorating tips
   (Found in cooking stores or hardware stores.)

DIRECTIONS

Use an electric mixer to whip the shortening, margarine, and vanilla. Add the sifted sugar one cup at a time, beating well after each addition. The frosting will be very stiff and dry.

Add the milk. Whip until light and fluffy.

Divide the frosting into several small bowls, and add different food colors. Stir the colors into the frosting. Put the frosting into pastry bags that have decorating tips. Fold down the tops of the bags.

The children will soon learn how to squeeze the frosting onto their gingerbread boys, adding a variety of other decorations of their choice.

COLORED SUGAR

Put a cup of granulated sugar in a jar with a lid. Add a few drops of food coloring. Shake the jar until the food coloring spreads through the sugar. (Children love to help with this step.) The sugar is ready to use. Make as many different colors in separate jars as you wish.

Epilogue

Dear Mrs. Dondiego,

    Thank you very much to come in and help us make crafts. I really appreciate you coming in and wasting your time to be with us.

Sincerely,
Meredith W., Age 9

INDEX